Blog to Book & Beyond

A New Path to Publishing Success

Blog to Book & Beyond

A New Path to Publishing Success

by

Tom Masters

Orion Wellspring, Inc.

Seattle

First edition, first printing September, 2010
Copyright © 2009 by Tom Masters, All rights reserved.
Published by Orion Wellspring, Inc., Seattle, WA 98109
(206) 931-4656

ISBN-13: 978-0-9794614-0-8
ISBN-10: 0-9794614-0-5
9 8 7 6 5 4 3 2 1
Printed and bound in the United States of America.

Notice of Liability

Notice of Rights

Trademarks

Orion Wellspring, Inc.
20 Blaine St.
Seattle, WA 98109

Contents

Introduction

Anya Peters did not start out to be a writer. She had a difficult childhood that was scarred by abuse. In the summer of 2005, financial and emotional difficulties left Peters living in her car. During the nine months she lived in her car, she began blogging about her experiences on a site called *Wandering Scribe*. She used computers in Internet cafes to make her blog posts. In February 2006, she began writing her blog which quickly acquired a worldwide readership. A month later she was featured in a *New York Times* article. This in turn was picked up by other media and more attention followed. She was signed by Curtis Brown, one of Britain's largest literary agencies, which soon had landed Peters a book deal with HarperCollins.

This rapidly evolving sequence of events put her in an unusual position. As the BBC News described it, "Still living in her car, she found herself in the surreal position of being homeless and taking calls offering her book deals, with reports about her blog appearing in papers such as the New York Times and Le Monde."

Her book, *Abandoned: The True Story of a Girl who Didn't Belong*, has been a solid success and allowed her to return to a more normal life. While her circumstances were extraordinary, Anya Peters' blog to book path to publication is becoming more commonplace. The blogosphere is proving a fertile hunting ground for publishers searching out new talent.

Blogging, one of the Web's earliest forms of social media, is now a part of our culture. Blogs are a powerful way to exchange ideas, hold conversations with others and influence attitudes.

The first blogs appeared only a few years ago; today there are over 100 million blogs and counting. Blogs are used by political candidates to debate issues, by consumer advocates to evaluate products and services, and by individuals to share their everyday experiences. Blogs are also emerging as a tool for authors to build an audience for their work.

There are many advantages to blogging for writers, especially unpublished authors. Blogging helps you establish an audience. It also helps you hone your writing style and establish a regular discipline of writing. Blogs are also measurable. You can track who comes to your blog, what they view, how long they spend there, and through the comments they leave, their reactions to what you have written. These statistics represent important information for publishers who want to know that you can attract and engage readers. Finally, blogs can be a great marketing platform for your work.

The proliferation of low cost or free, user-friendly tools makes it easy for anyone to blog. But many find that becoming a successful blogger—a blogger with a growing audience—is easier said than done. Blogging has much in common with a magazine. It is one part writing compelling articles on a schedule, one part marketing and promotion, and, if you are thinking about earning income from your blog, one part advertising and sales. Too many bloggers start with a great deal of enthusiasm, but quickly lose momentum. To avoid running out of steam, you need to complement your passion and excitement with a considered and disciplined approach. *Blog to Book & Beyond* focuses on this type of planning and execution.

In *Blog to Book & Beyond*, you will discover:

- How authors are using blogs
- How to use the different types of blogging tools
- Blog writing techniques that attract readers
- Tips to help you reach more readers
- How to track and measure your readership
- How to turn your blog into a bestselling book

To get the most out of *Blog to Book & Beyond*, you only need to know how to use a web browser and have some familiarity with basic web search tools such as Google.

The resources in the appendices provide a comprehensive list of tools and references to help as you get started. Blogging, like most technologies, comes with a host of specialized terms. With this in mind, a Glossary is provided to help you navigate this growing lexicon.

For additional resources and updates about blogging and its uses, please visit the companion blog to this book, *Future Perfect Publishing* at http://www.futureperfectpublishing.com.   Please feel free to send your suggestions and comments.

Blogging offers a powerful way to communicate your ideas and connect with an audience, but it takes patience and planning to realize the power of this new writing medium. *Blog to Book & Beyond* helps you understand and apply techniques to make your blog stand out from the crowd and, in the process become a successful author.

1
Blog to Book Revolution

Shauna James started blogging in 2004 because she had a problem. She had just been diagnosed with celiac disease – an allergy to gluten. Gluten is a substance added to food as a preservative and is nearly ubiquitous in the food supply. Shauna found that she needed to radically change her diet, but didn't know how. She began blogging about her search for information and soon attracted a large following. By the spring of 2007, her blog readership had grown to over 40,000 unique visitors per month.

The success of her blog, which she had named *Gluten Free Girl* (www.glutenfreegirl.com), captured the notice of John Wiley & Sons, a large New York book publisher. Based on her large audience and the engaging style of her blog posts, Wiley signed her to a book contract. She announced the forthcoming book to her readers, who embraced it enthusiastically. By the time of publication, her book had set a new pre-order sales record at Amazon.

This story illustrates how blogs are changing the nature of book publishing. Blogs have become a new medium. David Sifry, CEO of *Technorati*, the largest blog search engine, points out that twelve of the top 100 media properties in the U.S. (in terms of audience size) are now blogs. Using blogs, authors can tap the power of blogging to build an audience while they write. And they can apply the technologies of search marketing and social networking to market their work.

The Blogging Medium

Blogs are one more step along the evolution of web-based social media that began soon after the birth of the Internet. The first blogs were essentially online diaries or extensions of the "What's New?" section of websites, where entries were shown in *reverse* chronological order. Today, the use of blogs has expanded well beyond online journaling.

The term "weblog" was first used in 1997 and later shortened to "blog." For a time, blogs remained primarily components of conventional websites. Then, the first *blogging tools* appeared in 1999. A blogging tool is a software package that makes it easy to create and manage a blog. Some of the early tools included *Open Diary*, *LiveJournal*, *Diaryland* and *blogger.com* (which was later purchased by *Google*). During this time, developers added features that made it easier for blogs to link to each other.[1] Blog search engines appeared soon after.[2] By 2001, key technical innovations and market factors were in place for an explosion in blogging:

- Low cost, user-friendly blogging tools
- A critical mass of active bloggers
- Broad Internet adoption
- Robust blog search tools that made it easy to find blogs on any topic
- A syndication protocol (RSS) that, in combination with RSS reader / aggregators, made it possible to subscribe to blogs and eliminate tiresome searching.

In the early 2000's, the growth in blogging was fueled by technical savants talking to each other about the latest technologies, news stories reported by citizen journalists, and politics. In particular, Howard Dean's 2004 presidential campaign brought the power of the Internet and blogging, as tools of political influence, into the consciousness of Americans.

The next phase of blogging growth is in the area of organizational blogging. Companies, governmental agencies and not-for-profit organizations are exploring the use of blogs to communicate more directly with customers, employees and other stakeholders.

There are several factors driving the popularity of blogs and blogging today:

- Simplicity
- Flexibility
- Focus

- Syndication

Each of these factors plays a role in explaining why blogs represent a new type of media – a *social* media.

Think about blogging as a way to have a web presence without the need for technical knowledge. In the past, anyone wanting to set up a website had to understand HTML or know someone who did. The wide availability of blogging tools that require no technical expertise makes blogging a preferred means of creating a web presence.

Originally, blog content was mostly text. Today's blogging engines now support a broader creative palette; not only text, but audio, graphics and video. As the technology expands to fit the demand, blogs are even incorporating tools such as online conferencing.

While the range of topics addressed by bloggers can run the gamut, most blogs are tightly focused on specific subject areas. This, combined with their frequent updates, makes them more visible to the search engines that routinely crawl the Internet.

Perhaps one of the most important features of blogs is their ability to be syndicated. Syndication is a way for readers of a blog to subscribe to its content. The content is then delivered to them automatically without the need to surf to the blog everyday. For now, think of syndication as a way for the blogger to easily reach a wide audience of readers with almost no additional effort.

All of these factors make blogging attractive to a broad segment of the population. Like other phenomena springing from the Internet, blogging was initially embraced by technically oriented individuals who wanted to communicate in new ways with each other about technology. As the less technically savvy computer user learned about blogging, non-technical applications developed.

A survey in 2008 by *Technorati*, showed the extent of the blogosphere; there were over 112 million blogs and 1.6 million blog posts daily. The growth of blogging has been nothing short of phenomenal (see Figure 1-1 below).

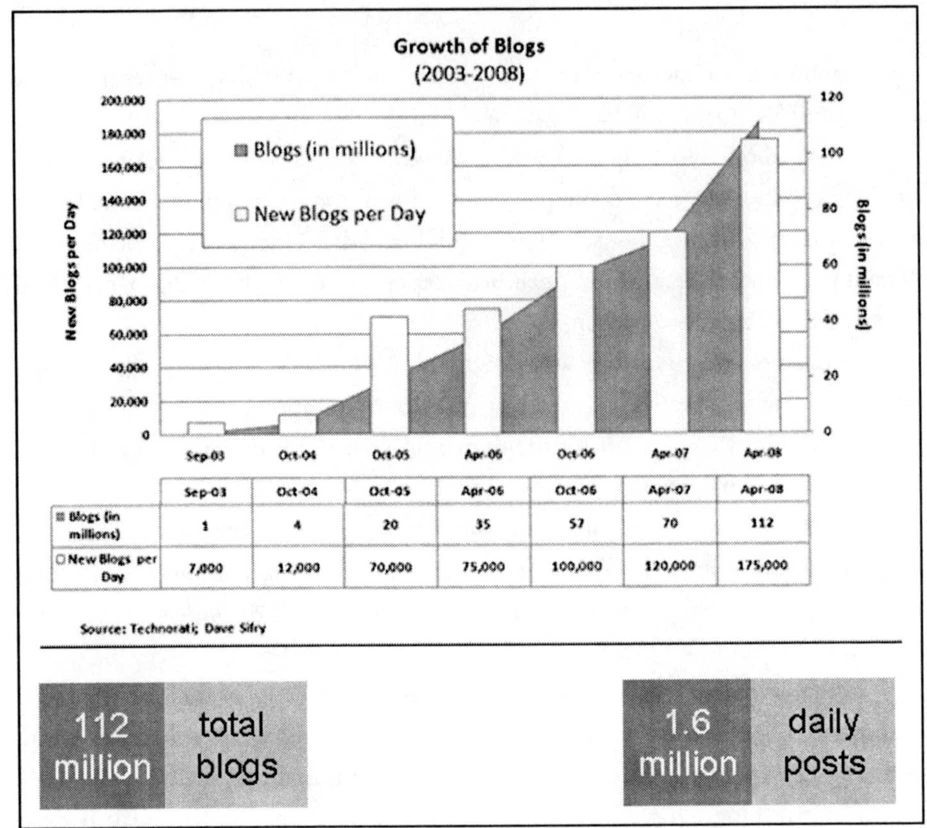

	Sep-03	Oct-04	Oct-05	Apr-06	Oct-06	Apr-07	Apr-08
Blogs (in millions)	1	4	20	35	57	70	112
New Blogs per Day	7,000	12,000	70,000	75,000	100,000	120,000	175,000

Source: Technorati; Dave Sifry

Figure 1-1 The Growth of the Blogosphere 2003-2008

The profile of today's blogger is much more mainstream. It is really everybody's game now. A survey conducted by the Pew Internet Study in the spring of 2008, revealed that 33% of internet users (the equivalent of 24% of all adults) say they currently read blogs, with 11% of internet users doing so on a typical day.[3] The survey also found that there is almost no gender gap in blog reading. Male and female internet users are equally likely to say that they read other people's blogs (35% for men, 32% for women).

Not surprisingly, fewer individuals are likely to write a blog. The Pew study found that 12% of internet users (representing 9% of all adults) say they ever create or work on their own online journal or blog. For a majority of bloggers, working on their blog is not an every-day activity: 5% of internet users blog on a typical day.

Book Publishing – Risky Business

The traditional world of publishing is governed by scarcity and cloaked in secrecy. Authors labor over their manuscripts, sometimes for years. The author enterprise is a lonely one. The research is compiled and the writing is perfected, frequently in a vacuum of feedback. Once the manuscript is completed, they may spend months or even years trying to interest publishers or agents in their work, often without success. This is especially true if the writer hasn't been published before or doesn't have a credible sponsor into the publishing world.[4]

The industry is controlled by gatekeepers jealously guarding access to scarce editorial, production and marketing resources. Publishers face enormous risks to bring a new title to market. Here are a few examples:

- Finding good product is difficult: Book publishing's success rate has been estimated to be 7-9 failures for every success.

- Long, highly uncertain publishing schedules: Manuscripts are often delayed or need extensive rework, pushing out launch dates and possibly missing important windows of opportunity.

- Little reliable market research available for new titles, categories: Until recently, there has been little objective data to guide product and market decisions.

- Margin pressure: Distributors often demand 55-70% of the suggested retail price of a book leaving less money available for marketing titles.

- Bookseller concentration: A few large chains, which focus more and more on best selling authors, dominate the retail channel.

- Best seller pressure: Most large publishing houses are now part of media conglomerates which must meet high quarterly earnings targets. This has shifted publishers' focus from building a reliable backlist to creating bestsellers. As a result, sales volume is now concentrated in fewer authors who can dictate unfavorable terms to publishers.

- Poor cash flow dynamics: Distributors typically pay late (anywhere from 120-180 days), and vendors collect early.

- Returns from booksellers average 30%: Bookstores essentially have books on consignment. Any unsold books can be returned to the publisher, at the publisher's cost.

- High marketing costs limit the amount of promotion given to most books: Book tours, advertising and access to traditional media are expensive. Publishers have put much of the marketing burden back on authors, who must pay for these efforts out of their advance.

The biggest risk a publisher faces is finding an author who has an audience of readers that will buy his or her book. Unsold books carry the costs of marketing, production, storage, shipment and ultimately, being pulped or remaindered.   Many publishers have left the task of selecting manuscripts for consideration to the judgment of trusted agents.   But even the most experienced agent may still have difficulty predicting how successful a specific author or title will be.

Gatekeepers are also found guarding access to publicity, e.g., book reviewers at influential publications or broadcast media outlets.   Buyers at wholesalers, distributors and retailers carefully control the flow of books to the finite and competitive retail bookshelf.   Publishers often have to buy their way into this sacred space with special book displays at the end of aisles ("end caps") and other expensive promotions.

There are alternative strategies available to publishers. Smaller publishers, who cannot afford such risks, have responded by focusing on niche markets, going to a fee for service model or becoming book packagers. Each of these strategies offers the publisher some safe haven from the risks presented by the traditional publishing model.

Focusing on a niche market allows an independent publisher to better identify and target the audience for the books they publish, build and leverage relationships with authors, and channel members who service that niche. Costs are predictable and their upside is primarily limited by the size of the niche.

In the fee for service model, the publisher agrees to publish an author's manuscript and perhaps provide some limited publicity and marketing assistance. The author bears all the financial risk; the publisher makes a prescribed profit margin, but generally has no further upside potential if the book becomes successful.

The other strategy publishers can use to lower their risk is to become a book packager. In this instance, the publisher pitches a book concept to a group of buyers who, if they agree to carry it, will pay for production costs plus a prescribed margin. In this model, there are no returns. Again, upside potential is sacrificed for a guaranteed profit on each sale.

The Transformation to Open Publishing

For many years, this presented a dilemma for would-be authors. Publishers didn't want to publish unknown authors. But without a publishing portfolio it was very difficult to get published.   Writers could turn to fee for service (or vanity) publishers. But this lacked credibility with the publishing establishment, booksellers and even other writers.

During the past decade, several developments have changed the traditional landscape of publishing. These include:

- Print on demand production technology
- Self publishing services
- Online booksellers like Amazon
- Blogs and other social media
- Book sales tracking services, e.g., Nielsen BookScan
- New formats and channels for books such as e-books that take advantage of our Internet culture

Taken together, these changes have opened up many new possibilities for authors and ushered in a new era of book publishing where objective data replaces guesswork and pulling strings.

Print on demand (POD) – Print on demand refers to digital printing technology which allows small volumes of books (even a single copy) cost effectively; essentially on demand as books are ordered.[5] (Another term, used in the industry, is short run digital printing.) The advantage is that it dispenses with the need for warehousing. Publishers can also use print on demand to handle orders for low volume books on their backlist. Per unit costs for print on demand books are higher than books printed on offset presses, but these days the quality is about even.

Self publishing services – Self-publishing services provide authors with the tools, technologies and services they need to get their book into production. In combination with print on demand, it is now easy for anyone to publish a book in small quantities at low cost. Many of the self-service publishing firms offer in-house or third party services to assist authors with cover design, interior design, content / copy editing and marketing. This is the first step towards the democratization of the book production. The explosion of books pouring from publishing services such as *Lulu*, *Blurb* and *iUniverse* portends a new, more open world of publishing. There seems to be an almost insatiable urge to publish. And the effects of technology-driven long tail economics is creating a new kind of publishing industry that will support a much wider range of product choices than in the past.

Many independent publishers started in business as authors who published their own work. Today, over 78% of all titles now come from independent publishers. The growth in independent publishers over the last 60 years has been dramatic, as these statistics published by Dan Poynter illustrate.[6]

1947: 357 publishers
1973: 3,000 publishers
1980: 12,000 Publishers
1994: 52,847 publishers
2005: 86,400+ publishers

Of the 86,400 publishers in 2005, there were only six large conglomerates and 3-400 medium sized publishers.

Online booksellers – Amazon.com's impact on bookselling is difficult to overestimate. Since it's inception in 1996, the online book retailer has steadily gained market share even as overall book sales have slowed into the low single digits. In his insightful book, *The Long Tail: Why the Future of Business is Selling Less of More*, Chris Anderson chronicles the manner in which Amazon has opened up a new, more democratic book sales channel for publishers of all sizes.

Blogs and social media – Blogging is a relatively new technology that allows anyone to publish on the Internet. In just a few short years, it has become immensely popular. *Technorati*, one of the leading blog search engines, has indexed over 100 million blogs. Topics covered are broad ranging and the demographics of bloggers and those who read blogs, as tracked by the Pew Internet Study, are becoming more mainstream.

The blogosphere is also becoming global. According to a survey conducted by Technorati, at the end of 2006, 33% of blog posts were in Japanese and 10% were in Chinese. One can imagine that the majority of posts may one day be in Chinese given that country's rapidly developing technology infrastructure, its enthusiastic embrace of the Internet and its huge population.

Many traditional media outlets are now using blogs to reach out to members of their audience. In fact, twelve of the top media properties in the US (in terms of audience size) are now blogs. All of this has led to an increase in the value of blogs as media properties. The top ranked blogs have acquired significant monetary value as their popularity has grown. This is due to the potential audience they can deliver to advertisers and marketers.[7]

Books sales tracking services – *Nielsen BookScan*[8] is a service that provides weekly point-of-sale data and functions as a central clearinghouse for the book industry. Its subscribers can access reports from a wide variety of perspectives. The firm provides a continuous market measurement of retail book sales based upon electronic sales data analysis. The service collects point-of-sale information from a large number of retailers and makes this information available to the industry. In a typical week, sales of over 300,000 different titles are collected, coded and analyzed, and reported out to retailers, publishers and the media.

In the past, consumers relied upon bestseller lists to identify which titles were leading in sales. The preparation of these lists was not public and their objectivity and accuracy was suspect. The availability of hard sales data from a trusted third party will guide publishers in making better title acquisition and marketing decisions.

New book formats and channels – In the past couple of decades, a number of book formats have emerged. The audiobook, which can be purchased on tape or CD, or downloaded to your computer, has proven an especially durable and popular format for consumers with long commute times.

A format related to the audiobook is the download of titles delivered as serial podcasts. These can be free or made available on a subscription basis.

Books are now available for rent using the Netflix model. Subscribers pay a monthly fee and may rent 3-4 books at a time. As they finish a book, they return it in a prepaid mailer. Books are selected from a website which features the entire catalog.

The electronic book (or e-book) has been touted as the future of the book. It has the advantages of portability, requires no shelf space and can be easily downloaded to an e-book reader. The e-book has struggled, however, because of the cost of readers, incompatibility of formats between readers, and the quality of the onscreen reading experience. No doubt adoption will grow as the technology improves and more titles become available in e-book format.

Books have more recently become available in other electronic formats, e.g., delivered in e-mail, or on mobile phones. Companies such as *DailyLit* are offering readers the ability to get books delivered in a serial format via e-mail. Subscribers to these services can select the frequency and length of installments they receive for titles they have chosen.

Summary

Just as Amazon and other online booksellers have created bookstores with essentially unlimited shelf space that can accommodate a much wider selection of titles and authors, print on demand and self-publishing services makes it easy for anyone to publish a book in small quantities at low cost. Many offer in-house or third party services to assist authors with cover design, interior design and content / copy editing. This is the first step toward the democratization of the book production. The availability of low cost marketing and promotion techniques via the web allows independent publishers to ramp up book sales outside of the traditional bookstore channel. This represents a major step forward in the democratization of book marketing. The last leg of the journey to a fully open publishing model could be heralded by the launch of the Espresso Book Machine from On Demand Books LLC, a system which can bind and print a book in 5-7 minutes.[9] This may eliminate the overhead of inventory and distribution altogether. The book remains digital all the way to the point of sale. One could imagine bookstores downloading, binding and printing a book while the customer has a latte--the *infinite* bookshelf comes to your local bricks and mortar bookstore.

Technology is creating new opportunities in book publishing. There is an exciting future for the book, one of mankind's most amazing and durable inventions. As the democratization of publishing progresses, prepare for a renaissance in book writing, publishing and reading.

2
How Writers Benefit from Blogging

As we saw in Chapter One, the popularity of blogs has soared in the last few years. There are now over 100 million blogs tracked by *Technorati*, a popular blog search engine. According to demographics collected by the *Pew Internet Study*, blogs are mainstream and represent virtually every audience and topic area.

Blogs offer authors several key advantages.

- Blogs are a special type of website. Due to their generally heavy use of links and their relatively frequent updates, blogs tend to rank well in search engine results. This makes them an attractive tool for building an audience around your content.

- Blogs are very similar to books in structure, making it easier to transition from blog to book.

- Blogging offers you the opportunity to establish a relatively painless writing discipline. Blog posts are typically just a few short paragraphs, about 300-500 words in length. Posting with regular frequency lets you build your book's content in a measured and disciplined manner. As your blog's readership builds and you realize you are writing for an audience that wants to consume your content, the task becomes easier.

- Blogs are very measurable. You can track your readership to a very specific degree. This is important because having an audience and knowing who your readers are is valuable information for publishers. The statistics you collect can also help you decide which content is popular and valuable, and which might be better omitted from your book.

- Finally, because it is easy to search and find blogs discussing the topics you are writing about, the blogosphere is an effective medium in which to market your completed work.

In this chapter, you will learn how all of these factors can help you establish and grow your audience, *while you write*.

Blogs Help People Find You

Building readership for your blog is all about *authority*; that is, getting others to link to your site, especially others with lots of their own inbound links. In fact, graphs of the blogosphere show a wide variance in the size of blogs as measured by the number of their inbound links. But is there any logic to all this business about links and authority?

Actually, quite a bit (for example, see Duncan Watts' book *Six Degrees*). One term used for this area of study is *network science*, which has its origins in the branch of mathematics known as *graph theory*. One of the most interesting discoveries about social networks is that they follow a power law distribution rather than a normal distribution. What does that mean?

Many, if not most, measurable properties associated with human behavior tend to cluster in a nice bell shaped curve around an average value. This reflects a random variation. However, social networks do not display randomness. For example, studies done of Internet linkages, including Dave Sifry's analysis of authoritative blogs,[10] show a decidedly different pattern. Consider a blog as a node in the greater blogosphere with some number of other nodes, k, linking to it. If you draw a graph showing the number of nodes of size k, for each value of k, it looks vastly different than a normal (bell shaped) curve. See the comparison below.

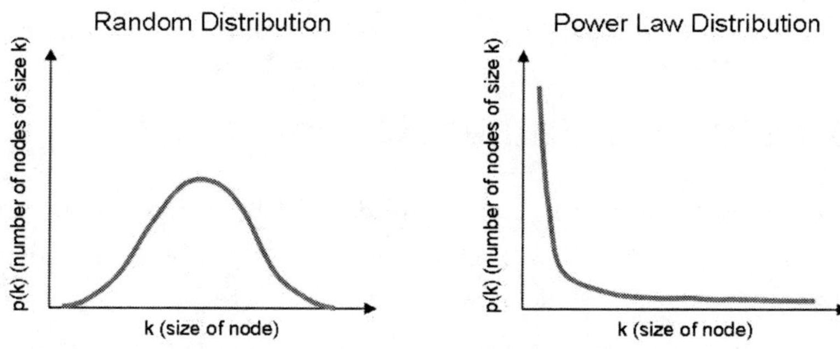

Figure 2-1 Random vs. power-law distribution

All this really means is that there are lots of blogs with few inbound links and not very many blogs with lots of inbound links. And the numbers change by some exponential power, for example powers of 10. Studies have shown that this is true of all social networks, even the offline variety (see *Linked* by Alberti-Laszlo Barabasi).

Blogging Helps Build Writing Discipline

Authors often struggle with writer's block. They simply can't get into the habit of writing on a regular basis and getting their work down on paper. Part of the problem in the past has been that writing is a lonely undertaking. The writer sits facing the blank paper or computer screen, alone with his or her thoughts. Part of the problem is that there is no sense of an audience. It is easier to create something when you know there is an audience waiting for what you have to write.

Blog posts can be any length, but probably average in the neighborhood of 300-5000 words. Blogging helps you steadily build your manuscript in these small chunks. A writer blogging every day can create 50,000 words in about 100-160 days, depending on their daily output.

Whether you blog every day, three times a week or just once a week, blogging helps you develop the habit of writing on a regular schedule. The nice part of this discipline is that you are building your audience at the same time.

You can see the growth in your readership every time you review your blog statistics and this can provide the motivation to keep writing.

Blogs Help You Gather Research

Some writers use their blog not only to develop book content, but also as a research vehicle for the book that is based on the blog. An article in *Computerworld*[11] describes a project by two authors, Gregg Taylor and Lori Thiessen, writing about the new group of nomadic workers operating from venues like Starbucks. The book and the blog are both called *Coffee Shop Office.*

Blogs offer many ways to gather research for your book. You can ask your readers questions to solicit their comments and feedback. You can set up polls and surveys, and then share the results with your readers in a blog post. You can also get your readers into the act of creation by asking them for stories that can be shared.

Your Blog is a Book in Disguise

The first thing to understand about a blog is that it is just a special type of website. Like websites, blogs have a web address or URL (universal resource locator). But blogs have a number of characteristics that make them unique and compelling. For example, you will notice that most blogs are full of links. Links are in the posts themselves, maybe linking to earlier posts, and there are links to other blogs.

Blogs also tend to have more of a "personality" than traditional websites. Unlike many websites, blogs strongly reflect the knowledge, experience and makeup of the author. Blogs are updated much more frequently than a conventional website, in many cases on a daily basis. Finally, blogs are designed to be more like a conversation versus a billboard or order form.

Below are some of the structural components you will find on most blogs.

Title. Generally the title of a blog is prominently displayed at the top of the blog page and may have an eye catching graphic. The title may be explicit, giving you a clear idea of what the blog is all about, e.g., *ProBlogger.* Or the blog author may decide to use a catchy name that is easy to remember, e.g., *Boing Boing* or *Gizmodo*.

Subtitle. Often blogs have a subtitle which the author uses to convey more strongly what the blog is about.

Posts. One of the first things you will notice when you go to a blog is that it is a sequence of entries or "posts," arranged in *reverse* chronological order so that the most current entries appear at the top of the page. Generally, posts have a title that reflects its content and a date (supplied automatically by the blogging platform when the post is published).

In this sense, reading a blog feels like reading someone's diary to see what they are thinking on a particular day. This immediately sets up a connection with the author. Unlike a website, this feels more personal, as if you are in the presence of another person.

Posts can contain links to external sites, documents or previous posts. Posts may include pictures, as well as audio or video clips. These tend to make a post more interactive, informative and / or entertaining.

Author information. Blogs often contain a short paragraph about the author and sometimes a picture. Authors will often provide their e-mail address to encourage further interaction with their readers.

Pages. Blogs will typically feature a main page that shows the posts. However, it is common to find blogs today with multiple pages. For example, a blog may feature a page that talks in depth about the blog author or the purpose of the blog. Or, for blogs with a more commercial orientation, there may be a page which describes products or services offered by the author or his / her organization.

You can create a blog page that provides information about your book, once it has been published, including:

- Book description
- Testimonials
- Author events
- Press releases
- Book reviews
- Ordering information

In this sense, your blog transforms from a vehicle for creating your manuscript into a powerful marketing engine.

Categories. Many blogs today feature *categories*. Categories allow you to label or tag posts that help classify them for readers. For example, if you have a blog that talks about orchids, you might have categories that signify particular species of orchids, how to grow orchids, the value of rare orchids, exhibiting orchids, and so on. Categories make it easy for your readers to find particular posts of interest. Blogs with categories will typically display those categories along the side of the blog, with a count of the number of posts in that category. You may assign a post to multiple categories depending on its content, and for this reason, categories help to amplify the apparent amount of content on your blog.

Permalinks. One of the most important types of links associated with a blog is the *permalink*. The term permalink is shorthand for "permanent link." This is the unique URL, or web address, of a single post. With its permalink, you can access any post, even after it is moved into the archives. This is how one blog links to a post in another blog.

Blogroll. A blogroll is a list of links to other sites or blogs. You may have discovered some great resources for your blog topic and the blogroll is a simple way to share them with your readers.

Comments. This is an area where visitors to the blog can leave comments on your posts. Some blogging tools display the comments associated with a post automatically. Sometimes, the reader has to click on a link to see the comments. Generally, these tools also show the number of comments for a post. Most blogging platforms give you the option to turn off comments. However, comments are an excellent way to connect with your audience. We discuss when and how to use comments in Chapter 5.

Archives. Typically, the amount of content produced on a blog grows with time. Usually blogs only display a handful of the most recent posts. Older posts move to the blog's archives. Most blogs provide one or more ways to access archived posts and their associated comments. For example, with a time-based method to access archived posts, a visitor can click a link labeled with the month and year and view the posts made during that time period. Another popular organization of previous posts is by category (see above). In this model, the author assigns category keywords to a post. These categories are displayed on the blog page. When a visitor clicks on the category name, he or she can view the posts tagged with that category label. Some blogging platforms provide a mechanism to list the titles of the most popular posts, usually organized in descending order of popularity. This lets the reader quickly see what other visitors have deemed to be the most useful or interesting posts. Usually posts older than some given amount of time, say a month, are automatically moved into the archives.

Subscriber links. As mentioned in *Chapter 1*, one of the most important features of a blog is its ability to be syndicated. Using a technology called Really Simple Syndication (RSS), visitors can subscribe to your blog. Then, with a desktop application tool called an RSS reader or a web-based feed service, they can view your posts automatically without having to surf over to your blog. Most commercially available blogging tools provide options that allow you to enable RSS feeds for your blog. (See *Appendix A* for a more detailed description of Really Simple Syndication.)

Widgets. A number of companies have developed "blog accessories," small pieces of software which perform useful functions for the blog's reader or author. These accessories are commonly called "widgets." For example, there are widgets which allow your readers to add a link to your blog or post on a bookmarking site such as *Digg*. Another widget might give you the ability to easily poll your readers about a subject. Another might allow you to syndicate your blog and alert mobile subscribers when you post a new entry. (For a sampling of the widgets available for bloggers, go to *WidgetBox* at www.widgetbox.com.)

In terms of its structure, you can think of a blog as a kind of online book. For example, a blog has a title and / or subtitle that reflect the content within. Blog posts can be organized into categories which serve as a kind of table of contents to classify and group related material. Blog posts, typically 300-500 words in length each, represent the raw content of a book. If you blog regularly and frequently, you will be surprised at how quickly your body of content builds up. Before long you may have one or more "book equivalents" worth of content in your blog. Links within posts or on the blogroll serve as footnotes or endnotes, acting as references to source material. In all of these ways, a blog is a book in disguise.

The comparison between book structure and blog structure is summarized in the table below.

BOOK	BLOG
Title	Title
Subtitle	Subtitle
Author biography	Author information
Topics	Categories
Content	Posts
Footnotes and endnotes	Links
Photographs, illustrations	Digital photos, drawings

Table 2-1 – Comparison of book and blog structures

The similarity in structure between a blog and book is interesting. But why should you want to use a blog to write a book? The primary reason is that a blog can help you attract an audience for your book while you are writing it.

Blogs Help Build Your Readership

How do you attract people to your blog? Initially, through searches individuals make on popular search engine sites like *Google*, *Yahoo* and *MSN*. By using popular keywords in your blog title, subtitle, categories and posts, your blog will begin to turn up in these searches. You can discover these keywords using special software called keyword discovery tools[11] or simply checking out popular blogs in your topic area and seeing what terms they use most often. For more information on keyword discovery, see Appendix C, *Keyword Research*.

The more you blog and the more others discover and link to your blog content, the higher your blog site will rank in search results. This means greater traffic for you blog. Your blog content acts as a magnet for searches in your subject area. Links made by others to your blog and its posts act as highways that readers follow to your content. The more pathways your blog accumulates over time, the greater the probability new readers will find your blog.

Blogs Help Track Your Audience

Blog software usually provides a basic set of statistics that allow you to track important information such as number of visitors, pageviews, referring sites and average time spent by each visitor. Pageviews and comments left by visitors for specific blog posts provide an indicator of popular content. This fact makes blogs an excellent way for you to field test and select material to be included in your book. Why is this important?

Most publishers have difficulty quantifying the readership for a title and, for this reason, are generally averse to taking a risk on an unpublished author. By developing your book around the content of a blog, you have the opportunity to share the metrics you have collected with prospective publishers and demonstrate that you know to attract an audience. We will discuss this in more depth in Chapter 7, *Pitch Your Book with Metrics.*

Blogs Allow You to Fine Tune Content

Besides using your blog metrics to characterize your audience, you can also use them to identify the most popular content. Many blogging tools, e.g. Wordpress, show you the breakdown of important information like page views by individual post. This makes it easy to spot content that draws the most interest from your readers. When creating a book from your blog, you can use this data to filter out content that doesn't seem to draw much response. In Chapter 7, *Pitch Your Book with Metrics,* we'll look at specific examples of statistics you can use to measure your content.

Blogs are Powerful Marketing Tools

Once you have cultivated an audience, you can transform your blog into a great marketing platform. For example, you can promote your book on a special page of your blog, featuring your bio, a book description, excerpts, press releases and testimonials. Thus your blog can double as a book website. You can also promote your book to a wider audience by arranging a blog tour. A blog tour is a series of scheduled guest appearances on related blogs, where you have the opportunity to talk about your book.[12] This is a low cost, high impact method to discover new readers for your work. We will discuss book marketing in the blogosphere in more detail in Chapter 8, *Go on a Blog Tour* and Chapter 9, Make *a Book Trailer*.

Blogging is a low risk, low cost way to build your audience while you are developing your work. Once your work is completed, you can use the blog to promote your finished book to that same audience. (Note that it not necessary to announce you are turning your blog content into a book prior to finishing your work.)

Summary

In this chapter, we examined the benefits of blogging for writers. Blogs:

- Are excellent vehicles to quickly build an audience for your work
- Mirror the structure of a book
- Help you build writing discipline
- Provide a great way to gather research with the help of your blog audience
- Help you track your readership
- Guide you in the selection of the best content for your book
- Serve as a powerful marketing tool for your book

Once the blog is in place, its content acts as a magnet, attracting readers through search engines. Whether you are publishing independently or trying to sign on with a traditional publisher, blogging can be the key to your success. Many publishers now view the blogosphere as a fertile ground to find promising writers. Why? As an author who blogs, you can demonstrate that you have an audience and quantify its extent; this is attractive to risk-averse publishers.

Using your new understanding of the overall structure and functioning of blogs, the next chapter presents an approach for planning your blog with the specific intention of using it to build an audience for your work. A well-planned blog is crucial to developing a strategy for building your readership.

3
Setup Your Blog

In the last chapter, you learned how you, as a writer, can benefit from blogging. Now it is time to actually set up your blog, begin posting, and build your readership. There are several important things to take into account when you create your blog.

Factors in Choosing a Blog Platform

As with making any important decision, it is worthwhile to take your time. There are many competing blog platforms on the market. While you can change your blog platform at a later time, there are usually some costs associated with such transfers. There are, of course, potential costs in switching from a free, hosted blog to a self-hosted blog, e.g., domain registration, monthly hosting fees, etc. Changing your domain also has implications on search engine traffic. It can diminish your readership and affect your blog ranking. So it is worth the investment of time to do your research and find a blog platform that will meet your needs for a long time. Below are factors you should consider before selecting a blog platform.[12]

Goals. Reviewing the goals you have for your blog will help guide your blog platform selection. Revisit your answers to these questions:

- Is blogging something you plan to do over the long term?
- What is the primary purpose of your blog?
- Is blogging more of a hobby for you or are you using it as part of a business or profession?
- Do you plan to put ads on your blog?

The level of sophistication of blogging platforms can vary widely. Find a platform that has the features and tools to suit your requirements, both now and in the future, as your blog grows.

Budget. As with most things in technology, blog platforms come with a variety of price points ranging from free to more expensive options. There are three main things that you might pay for:

- The blog platform itself
- Hosting for your blog
- Domain name

Different blogging platforms offer different levels of service. Some, like *Blogger.com* and *WordPress.com*, offer the platform, domain name and hosting for free. Others like *Wordpress.org* (note this is different from *WordPress.com*) offer the platform for free, but you then need to find and pay for your own hosting and domain name. Others, like *MovableType*, charge for a license for the platform which depends on how many blogs you have and whether they will have a commercial, personal, educational, or not-for-profit use. *MovableType* also has a free version which requires you to arrange and pay for your own domain name and hosting.

Other costs you might factor in at this early stage include:

Design. All platforms come with free templates (some more professional looking than others), but if you want a more customized look, you will either need to have some design skills, know someone who does, or be willing to pay for a design.

Blog tools / metrics. There are any number of tools you can pay for to help you become a successful blogger. These might include stats packages (again you can get free ones but can also pay for more features), and offline blog posting tools. If you are a beginner you might not need any of these, but down the road you might find them useful.

Your technical capabilities. This is a crucial factor to consider when choosing a blog platform. If you have never had any experience in creating a blog or website before and are not a technologically-minded person, there are some blog platforms and set-ups that are much more suited to your needs. If you know a few of the basics, or at least are willing to learn them, your platform choices are broader.

The other option is to find someone who is a "techie" to help you out (either paid or as a friend). One of the great things about blogging is that there is a wonderful communal knowledge and many forums dedicated to helping people get the most out of their chosen platforms.

Types of Blogging Platforms

Once you consider your goals and available budget for the blog, select one of the two available basic platforms:

- Hosted blog
- Standalone

Hosted Blog Platform

A hosted platform[13] will typically provide you with everything you need to get your blog up and running quickly: ready-made blogging software, easily configurable options and a set of templates from which to choose. One other attractive feature of the hosted blog platform is that it is usually very cheap or free. Examples of popular hosted platforms are *Blogger.com*, *WordPress.com*, *TypePad, LiveJournal,* and *MSN Spaces.*

These systems are 'hosted' blog platforms because they 'host' your blog on their own domain. After what is usually a relatively easy set-up process, they will give you a web address (URL) that will usually be some combination of their own URL and the name of your blog. For example, your blog on *WordPress.com* blog might be called **RealCoolGadgets** and would be listed as www.realcoolgadgets.wordpress.com. You can see the structure of that address has two elements—the blog's name first followed by the *WordPress.com* extension. This means that this blog is being 'hosted' by *WordPress.com* as opposed to you, the blogger, having to organize and pay for that.

Below are some of the advantages of having your blog on a hosted platform:

Inexpensive. As mentioned above, most hosted options are free.

Easy to set up. Most blogs on a hosted platform can be set up in minutes. You typically enter some basic information about your blog, set some options (e.g., whether you enable RSS syndication) and then select a template design from a gallery. Hosted blog platforms are ideal if you do not know, or are not interested in, dealing with the technical aspects of blogging.

Simple to manage. Hosted blogs make it easy to enter and format text, create links, add images and preview / publish your posts. Many of them have content entry interfaces reminiscent of the toolbars you find in Microsoft Word™. Publishing requires little more than clicking a button once you enter your content. Generally you see the results quickly.

Updated Automatically. When the blog platform software is enhanced, your blog will automatically get the updates. Instead of having to upload new software onto a server, these updates happen much more seamlessly.

Indexed in Search Engines Quickly. One of the advantages of many hosted blog platforms is that they are put onto domains with good page ranks already. While your blog will not be indexed in search engines when you start, most bloggers notice that their blogs get picked up and ranked fairly quickly. In the long-run, they probably do not rank much higher than other blogs on standalone hosting, but they are a quick way to get into search engines.

Below are some of the disadvantages of being on a hosted blog platform. Most of these relate to the degree of control you have over your blog.

Less configurable. One of the key concerns about being on a hosted blog platform is the limitation on your ability to customize your blog. This does vary from platform to platform within the hosted options. For example, *WordPress.com* has fairly limited design options, *Blogger.com* does not give the option for categories, and *TypePad* has different options depending upon at which level you buy in.

Default design limitations. While this can be true for standalone blogging systems, many hosted blogs end up looking very similar to one another. This is because the default templates get used over and over again, and if you are a beginner, they can be difficult to adapt. *Blogger.com*, for instance, requires that you know CSS and HTML to edit your templates (something you need to know with other hosted platforms as well).

Less ability to control performance. When your blog is on a hosted platform, you may experience degraded performance or downtime when the platform is having problems, and there is very little you can do about it. If problems persist for an extended period, this can impact your readership and blog rankings.

Generic URL. Generally, when you use a hosted platform, the domain name of the hosting service takes precedence. Your blog name is usually shown as a subdomain of the hosting service. For example, the URL visitors would use to find your blog looks something like:

http://yourblogname.hostname.com

This is in contrast to having your domain in a more prominent position, as in:

http://www.yourdomain.com

Having your own URL can give your blog a sense of professionalism that is not possible with the URL choices to which you are limited on hosted platforms. While there are very successful blogs on hosted platforms, some bloggers believe that having your own URL is much more professional if you are using your blog in a professional way. Recently, WordPress began offering bloggers the option to reserve and use their own domain name with the WordPress hosted blog platform. It seems likely that WordPress competitors will soon follow suit. This has the potential to remove one major objection to using hosted platforms.

Upgrading to standalone can be tricky. One of the issues of starting out with a hosted platform is that if you later want to go with a standalone platform, you may have some work ahead of you to retain any traffic that your blog has built up to date. It is not impossible to do, but there are implications for changing domains later in terms of taking regular readers with you, having to climb the search engine rankings all over again, and redirecting traffic from one blog to another.

So, when should you consider using a hosted blog platform? If you do not want your own domain, are not too interested in tweaking the design of your blog, or getting all the latest plug-ins, then the hosted blog platform is a good choice. It provides an easy entry into blogging.

Standalone Blog Platforms

As discussed briefly above, the other type of blog platform is that which is hosted under your own domain / URL. Examples of standalone blog platforms include: *Moveable Type, WordPress.org, B2Evolution, TextPattern* and *Expression Engine.* A Google search on "blogging software" will turn up many others.

Again, some of the advantages of using a standalone blog platform are listed below.

Full control of design. With standalone blogs, you generally have a great deal of control over your blog's design.   Of course, those bloggers with little ability in this area may either need to use default templates (with the same limitations as the default templates of hosted blogs) or get other people, paid or unpaid, to help.

Adaptability. Standalone platforms (e.g., *WordPress.org*) are constantly being extended by their developer communities with plug-ins, small pieces of code which are installed after blog set up and add capability to the basic installation.

Low acquisition cost. Standalone platforms are generally free to operate. You do pay for your domain name and hosting fees, however, and some platforms charge license fees (generally several hundred dollars) if you have multiple blogs or use them for commercial purposes.

Your domain. Having your own domain name has a number of advantages. It is easier to remember, it is often perceived as being more professional, and it is easier to turn into a brand as you build your readership.

Some disadvantages of going the standalone platform route are listed below.

Complicated set-up. If you have limited technical abilities, you may find the complexity of setting up a standalone platform a bit daunting. It often involves arranging hosting, setting up databases, downloading the platform onto your own computer to make changes, and then uploading it via ftp transfer onto your web hosting server. Good tutorials exist for most of the platforms to help with this process, but you may still find it difficult. Alternatively, you can hire a professional blog designer to do the set-up and design for you. Or, you can find a web hosting service that will install your blog platform. Some platforms, e.g., *WordPress.org* and *MoveableType,* provide recommendations for hosting services that will do it for you.

Ancillary costs. With the standalone platform, the blog software itself might be free, but you need to factor in several other costs:

- Fees to register and maintain your own domain name (generally around ten dollars per year)

- Fees for your hosting service (typically ten to twenty dollars per month depending on the options you choose)

- Bandwidth charges—this is important if you store and play back podcasts (audio segments) or videos on your blog

- Costs of hiring professionals to help you set up and / or design your blog.

Updates. These blog platforms generally go through new versions over time. Updating from one to another may be as complicated as your original set-up and could result in problems with your blog if you do not know what you are doing.

Hosting issues. Just as with hosted blog platforms, the hosting services you use may experience problems from time to time. Here the phrase *caveat emptor* (buyer beware) applies. Whether you use a hosted solution or a standalone solution, it is important to back up and be aware that occasionally systems do go down. Do your research and choose a reputable host if you select the standalone route to ensure your blog gets maximum uptime.

When should you use a standalone blog platform?

Standalone blog platforms are ideal if you want a little more control or flexibility with your blogging. They can be configured to look and run very professionally. They can be configured in ways that are constrained only by your imagination. Of course, just because you go with a standalone blog does not ensure you will have the perfect professional-looking blog. In fact if you do not have the ability to set these blogs up correctly, or know someone who can, standalone blogs can be messy and unprofessional looking.

Getting Started – Hosted Blogs

If you have chosen a hosted blogging platform, the blogging software is already set up for you. Here are the steps you will need to follow to get started blogging.

Set up an account. This usually only requires you to supply a username and e-mail address. The e-mail address is used to send you a welcome mail with initial login information. Once logged in, you change your password to something you will remember. Note that hosted blogging platforms may vary in their account setup requirements, but this process is pretty typical.

Choose a theme. A theme represents the "look and feel" of your blog; for examples, the font, colors, graphics and other styling elements. The major blogging platforms tend to have a large number of themes to choose from. Some themes allow for a minor amount of customization; e.g. changing the graphic in the blog header with one of your own.

Configure your blog. While there are many configuration options for blogs, there are a few that deserve special attention before you start blogging.

- Adding pages
- Defining categories
- Adding links to your blogroll
- Enabling an RSS feed for your blog
- Deciding how to manage comments

Blogging platforms generally have a dashboard, an area where you control various elements of the blog. Many blogging platforms now offer the ability to have multiple pages. You can use these to provide additional, usually static information, for your readers. For example, you may want to have an About page that contains a short bio, or a Resources page with links to books, videos and other sites of interest for your readers.

Besides adding pages to your blog, it is important to define the categories. Remember that categories are the principal tool visitors use to find your archived blog posts.

The blogroll represents those sites or blogs which you feel will be useful for your readers. Many readers place a high value on these resources, in addition to the posts you provide on your blog.

Recall that RSS (Really Simple Syndication) is a way for readers to subscribe to your latest blog posts without having to surf to your site. Many individuals use RSS as a way to follow a large number of related blogs in a time efficient manner. Enabling RSS on your blog will help you retain interested, but busy readers.

Getting Started – Standalone Blogs

If you have chosen a standalone blog, you will have more work to do up front. These additional steps include:

Domain registration. This is the process of reserving your unique domain name for your blog site with a service like GoDaddy or with your website hosting provider.

Setting up a website account with a hosting provider. Generally this involves selecting a website package consistent with the requirements of the blogging software you are using, and establishing FTP (File Transfer Protocol) access to the site so you can upload your blogging software and content files.

Uploading and installing the blogging software to your website. Once you have acquired the blogging software you are going to use for your blog, you need to upload it to your website and follow the instructions of the blogging software provider to install it on the site. In some cases, you may need the assistance of the website hosting provider to change certain settings for your website.

Setting up and configuring your blog. This process usually involves the same steps as for a hosted blog with one notable exception. You may want to customize your chosen theme to a much greater degree. This may require the support of graphics design and / or web development professionals. The nature and scope of the customizations you can perform will vary according to the blogging software you have chosen.

Summary

This chapter explored two different types of platforms you can use to establish your blog. Which one you choose will depend on factors like:

- Blog profile, purpose, and aspirations
- Budget
- Technical capabilities

Each type of platform has its own distinct advantages and disadvantages. Select the option that you feel is the best fit with your skills and resources.

Table 4-1 below summarizes factors to consider in choosing a blogging platform:

FACTOR	HOSTED	STANDALONE
Acquisition cost	Free or low cost	Free or low cost
Support costs	None	Software updates Hosting Design costs Domain registration
Setup & maintenance	Easy	Can be complex
Design flexibility	Limited to templates	Not limited
Extensibility	Limited to platform updates	Not limited
Domain name	Restricted	Not limited

Table 3-1 Factors in choosing a blogging platform

Once your blog is set up, you are ready to begin posting and building an audience. The next chapter explores specific tools you can use to research your book project.

4
Do Research with Your Blog

One of the first things that a blog can do for you is produce source material and perform research for your book. Readers may share stories or information or provide links to other useful sites. You can also use the tools we have just learned about, like RSS, to keep track of what others who blog about similar topics are talking about.

In this chapter, we will briefly explore some of the ways you can use the blogosphere to help you with your book research.

Gathering Research with Your Own Blog

Many writers have begun to realize the power of blogs to help them perform research. When Robert Scoble and Shel Israel set out to write *Naked Conversations*, their highly successful book about how businesses are using blogs to talk with their customers, they decided to set up a blog to help them gather information and stories from readers.

As mentioned in Chapter 2, Gregg Taylor and Lori Thiessen are doing the same thing for their forthcoming book, *Coffee Shop Office*, about individuals who use their local coffeehouse as both a place to socialize and an office. The blog contains a summary of the book and has a survey that coffeehouse commuters can take. In an interview on *Future Perfect Publishing*, Lori explained their reasons for using blogs as a book research tool:[14]

"Setting up a website and the blogs seemed a no-brainer because much of our lives, social and business, are being carried out online. We wanted to connect firsthand with people who were using the coffee shop as their alternative or preferred office, and hear about their experiences. That's why there is a link on the website and the blogs to our online survey. We want to capture as much raw data on this work trend as possible.

"Gregg also felt that packaging the research material into manageable chunks, like posts of about 350 words, would make the book writing process a bit less daunting. We've been finding out that blog writing and book writing are two different animals. Writing the posts have been useful though, as a way to really focus in on a particularly juicy piece of information."

Another way to use your blog for book research is to encourage your readers to share stories that will later form the content of your book. One highly successful example of this approach is the blog *The Peter Rost Blog* (http://peterrost.blogspot.com). The blog's owner, Peter Rost M.D., uses the blog to give industry insiders a place to report stories of potential malfeasance by pharmaceutical companies. He developed a book, *Whistle Blower*, based in part on his own experiences in the industry, as well as other stories supplied by his readers. He has since published additional titles along the same lines— *Emergency Surgery* and *Killer Drug*.

One rich source of information for your book is the comments that readers leave on your blog. These comments can point you to new material or provide ideas for enhancing your book's content.

Research Your Book with RSS

Really Simple Syndication (RSS feeds) are discussed in Chapter 2 as way for readers to easily keep up with your latest blog posts without having to navigate to your site for new posts. You can also use RSS feeds as a research tool for your book. You simply subscribe to the blogs in your topic area that seem to regularly provide interesting information or points of view. It is an easy matter to subscribe to ten or twenty of these feeds and review the latest posts from these blogs in just a couple of hours.

There are numerous RSS feed readers available (simply do a *Google* search on "RSS readers" and you will have many to choose from). They come in three basic types:

- Desktop RSS feed reader
- Browser-based RSS feed reader

- Web-based RSS feed aggregator

Desktop RSS feed reader. The desktop feed readers are software programs that you install on your computer. They make it easy for you to organize your feeds into groups that share some common theme or topic. To subscribe, you generally type in the URL of the blog you wish to follow, add it to a group you specify, and you are ready to start receiving the latest posts from that blog. Most feeds provide 10-15 of the latest blog posts. Some desktop feed readers also integrate with e-mail programs such as Microsoft Outlook.

Browser based RSS feed reader. Many of the later version browsers (e.g., *Internet Explorer* or *Firefox*) now come with RSS feed readers built in. When navigating to a site with an RSS feed, the browser alerts you to this fact.   You can then select an option on the browser to subscribe. Both *Internet Explorer* and *Firefox* let you organize RSS feeds in much the same way you can with your favorite sites.

Web-based RSS feed reader. There are a number of sites, e.g., *Bloglines*, that aggregate RSS feeds and let you subscribe by visiting their websites and selecting the feeds you are interested in.

You should select the type of RSS feed reader that best suits your working habits and preferences.

Searching with *Google* Alerts

Much of the research you do for your book may involve online searches using search engines like *Google, Yahoo!* or *Bing!* *Google* provides a simple, but useful, tool for periodically re-running searches that have been productive.

To activate this feature, go to http://www.google.com/alerts and enter the following:

- Search keywords
- Type of search results you wish returned, e.g., news, video, blogs, etc. (note the default is comprehensive which returns every kind of result)
- How often you want the search performed
- Your e-mail address

Google will then run your search with the frequency <u>you</u> prescribed and return the type of search results <u>you</u> indicated for the keywords <u>you</u> input. You can always stop the searches by deleting the alert.

Getting the Scoop with Twitter

One other research tool that is becoming increasingly popular is *Twitter*, the micro-blogging service operated by a small technology company called Obvious (http://www.obvious.com). As of this writing, Twitter has over 30 million users.[15] Twitter is free; you can open a Twitter account by going to http://www.twitter.com and providing a name and password for your Twitter account, as well as your name and e-mail address.

Using Twitter is easy. You can search Twitter using keywords to find others talking about subjects you are interested in. If you find someone's Twitter posts enjoyable, you can "follow" them by clicking the **Follow** button. You will then automatically receive their updates on your own Twitter page. Generally, over time, others begin following your Twitter posts as well.

Twitter posts are tiny compared with regular blog posts; the Twitter software only allows you to enter posts of 140 characters or less. It was originally created as a way for you to update your friends and family on what you were doing. It is now being used by its members in other ways. For example:

- Plugging into the raw elements of news stories while they are unfolding, e.g., the protests against the Iranian election results in Tehran

- Live blogging at conferences and events

- Distributing news stories, for example, when the CDC used Twitter to quickly get updates out on the swine flu epidemic

- Mobilizing customers, like a bakery in San Francisco that updates local customers who follow its Twitter posts on when its sumptuous peach pies are coming out of the oven

Authors are also starting to mine Twitter to find potential stories, people to interview and background information for their book projects.

Summary

In this brief chapter, we have looked at four tools you can use to research your book:

- Your own blog
- RSS feeds from other blogs
- Google alerts
- Twitter

These tools are not only potent sources of material, but are invaluable as time savers for gathering and organizing information. The subject of online research is quite large. If you are interested in learning more about the tools and techniques of web-based research, an excellent reference is *Information Trapping: Real-time Research on the Web* by Tara Calishain (see the bibliography).

The next two chapters investigate audience building techniques for writers of both non-fiction and fiction.

5
Create a Non-fiction "Blook"

In previous chapters, you learned how blogs can help your writing projects. Now it's time to focus on how a book can actually be created from a blog. Different techniques are used for non-fiction and fiction books. We will first examine how to go from blog to book for a non-fiction work. Blogging is an especially powerful technology for the non-fiction author.

As used here, the term "blook" is a contraction for "blog to book" and refers to a printed book containing content which first appeared on a blog. It was first coined in 2006 by Bob Younger, the founder and CEO of *Lulu*. He established a contest which awarded prizes for blog to book stories. He called his award, the "Blooker Prize."

Blook Motifs

Blog to book stories are becoming more commonplace. We have chronicled a number of such examples, and you can find a virtual library of blog to book stories on Cheryl Hagedorn's *Blooking Central* (blooking.blogspot.com).[16] Some of these blog to book stories were serendipitous, but more and more writers, especially new authors, are being more intentional about converting their blogs into a printed title. There is more than one way to execute a blog to book strategy. Here is one attempt at a blook typology:

Standard blook. The standard blook is a book that originates from the content of a blog. This is the form of blook that you are likely to read about in the newspapers. A large publisher discovers a high traffic blog and offers the blog owner a book deal. Their rationale is that if the blog has an established audience and a topic in line with the publisher's market focus, it will have a high probably of strong book sales. However, it is not just a game for large publishing houses. An author may independently publish and market his or her title based on a blog. Low cost self-publishing and inexpensive Internet marketing techniques are making this an attractive option for new authors who are not shy about self-promotion.

One example of a traditional blook is the blog to book deal obtained by Julie Powell. In 2002, Ms. Powell announced her intention to attempt cooking every recipe in the Julia Childs cookbook, *Mastering the Art of French Cooking.* She later described the origins for the project in an interview: [17]

"On the eve of my thirtieth birthday, stuck in a dead-end secretarial job, living in a hideous apartment in Long Island City, Queens, and dreading what seemed like a life of terminal mediocrity, I came up with a panicked notion — to cook through all 524 recipes of Julia Child's *Mastering the Art of French Cooking*, in a year, and blog about it. *Julie and Julia* describes my efforts to hold on to my job, marriage, and sanity while blazing a nonsensical trail toward fulfillment, with Julia leading the way."

Her blog, called *The Julie / Julia Project* (http://blogs.salon.com/0001399/) documented her struggles to understand and duplicate the recipes. Her blog quickly attracted an enthusiastic and sympathetic audience.

In 2005 Little, Brown published *Julie & Julia*. The book, started as a blog, has sold nearly 100,000 copies. "There was a built-in audience," says Judy Clain, Executive Editor] of Little, Brown. She recalls how, at a 2005 New York book fair, a third of the people who came to claim one of 1,000 copies said "they 'know the blog' and have 'been waiting for the book.' Usually, you are handing out a book, and most people have never heard of the author or the book." [18] In August 2009, Sony Pictures released the film version of *Julie & Julia*, based on an adaptation by writer-director Nora Ephron and starring Meryl Streep as Julia Child and Amy Adams as Julie Powell.

Reverse blook. In this scenario, an author blogs the content from an existing manuscript. The author can use the blog to test content for a forthcoming title or a new edition of an already released book.

Podiobook. This is more of an audio blook. Here the author serializes his or her book into podcasts and uses a blog for audience feedback and book marketing. It is especially effective for fiction writers. Two of the best know podiobook authors are Scott Sigler and J.C. Hutchins. We will discuss fiction blog to book techniques in detail in the next chapter.

Crowdsourced blook. This is a rare blook, but every author's dream come true. Here, the blog is so popular that a community emerges and contributes content which eventually winds up being part of the publishing or marketing strategy for a title. In other words, build a community that helps you generate content and then publish it. The best known example is Frank Warren's *Post Secret* (www.postsecret.com).

Back in 2004, Frank Warren began a sociology project where he asked people to submit their secrets anonymously on a standard postcard. He would then select the most interesting post cards and publish them on his *Post Secret* blog (www.postsecret.com). The response to his request was overwhelming. Many of the post cards submitted for publication on his site are artistic creations. Since that time, Frank Warren has published four collections of these post cards; all of them runaway bestsellers.

Post Secret is the premier example of a blog (and a set of books derived from that blog) where nearly all of the content is generated by its readers.

As this new form of book development evolves, blog to book strategies will replace the traditional (and mostly ineffective) approach to getting a book published which involves submitting a manuscript to agents or publishers in hopes of getting it read and eventually published. Publishing is a risky business. Of the many risks, the first and biggest is signing an unknown author who may or may not be able to attract an audience for their title. An author who has a blog with an established audience is an attractive proposition. Publishers can assess the quality and appeal of the writing. The popularity of blog posts can be measured and ranked. We can see how the audience reacts to the content long before it is edited into book form.   In the case of a popular blog, the audience can be larger than the circulation of many magazines or newspapers.

Blooks are not just a publishing sideshow, or interesting examples of pluck and luck. They represent a significant part of the future of publishing in a world of consumer-generated media.

Structure Your Blog like a Book

Blooks, books based on a blog, are increasing in popularity. Authors, especially unpublished authors, can benefit from blogging their material first as a way to build an audience for their work. There are enough blog to book success stories now to make this an attractive option. Many of the early blook successes were more the result of serendipity than plan. This section provides an approach for authors who are intentional about creating a book from a blog.

Title. Use the same title and subtitle for your blog that you would like to use for your book. This has the advantage of allowing your blog to double as a book website after publication. Also, it makes it easy for your blog readers to find your new book.

Table of Contents. Layout out your blog categories to roughly correspond to the table of contents for your book. Using exactly the same titles for categories and chapters may not always work. Categories are generally a better guide to subjects rather than specific chapters. Also, some standard table of content names won't make any sense for a blog, e.g., *Introduction* or *Epilogue*. The idea is to have a rough one-to-one correspondence in mind so that when you produce your manuscript, you will be able to map your blog content to the right places in your book.

Chapter Content. Your blog posts become the content for your chapters; content tagged for a particular category can go in the corresponding chapter. If you have a post tagged for multiple categories, the flow of your content will probably dictate which chapter it lands in.

Bibliography. The links in your posts become your pointers to reference material that appears in a bibliography or set of end notes.

Visuals. Pictures, illustrations and graphs may present a bit more of a challenge. If the pictures you want to use in your book involve licensing or permissions, you may have to use substitutes on your blog (or go without) while you are negotiating.

Author Bio. Most blogs make it easy to share your bio, either as a blurb on your main blog page or as a separate page. Include your picture, as well as both a short and long form bio for yourself which can be incorporated later into your book. Only the short form bio should appear on the blog.

Content Strategies

Every blog will differ in the type of content used to engage readers. However, there are several common types of posts that writers of non-fiction can use effectively on their blook blogs. These include:

- Experiences. Everyone loves a good story conveyed from a new perspective. Using your own experiences or someone else's is a great way to keep your readers coming back for more.

- Interviews. Interviews are an effective way to get someone else to do the heavy lifting of writing a blog post. Send your prospective interviewee a brief e-mail requesting the interview. Introduce yourself, provide a link to your blog, explain why you are interested in interviewing him/her, and what the interview will focus on.   Be sure to indicate the number of questions you will be asking. It gives your interviewee a good way to judge the time investment required. Eight to ten questions is probably about the limit for most people. The person you interview will often link their own blog or site to yours following publication of the post.

- Reviews. If it is appropriate to your topic area, consider writing reviews of products or services your readers might find interesting.

- Lists. This type of post is engaging and easy to both write and read. It usually starts off with a title like, "Five Things to Check Before Buying Your Next Car" or "The Ten Biggest Mistakes Beginning Golfers Make."

- Tips & How-to's. Readers are usually interested in how to do something better, especially if instructions are given in a simple step-by-step manner. If you are writing a how-to book, this type of post is a definite 'must-have' in your blog.

- Surveys & Polls. Surveys and polls are popular ways to get your readers to share their opinions or information. There are many plug-ins available to make the task of asking and analyzing survey questions painless. The key is to have short and unambiguous questions that are of interest to your audience.

- Guest bloggers. Why do all the writing yourself? If you know some individuals who have a good knowledge of your subject and would be agreeable to it, ask them to write an occasional blog post under their own byline. If they have a blog of their own, they will probably link to their guest post on your blog and bring you more traffic.

- Comment threads. As we mentioned earlier, comment threads are a good indicator of what gets your readers' attention. Comments can often be suggestive of new blog (and potentially book) material.

Establish an Editorial Calendar

An editorial calendar is a simple device to help you organize and stay on track with your blogging. It shows you a time sequence (usually a month in length) of the next set of blog posts. You can make each item on the list as detailed as you want, but generally a title and short description is a sufficient reminder. Use either a simple list with a date for each item, or an actual calendar. (If you want to keep your editorial calendar in digital form, a number of calendar templates are available for Microsoft Word from Microsoft's website at http://www.microsoft.com.)

Preparing an editorial calendar helps you think through not only the content you are going to blog about in the coming month, but also the types of blog posts you might want to use. Mixing up the type of blog posts you do makes your blog more interesting for readers. It is easy to hit a wall with blogging. Here are a few suggestions:

1. Get an RSS feed reader and point it to sites that talk about things in your topic domain. This often provides great ideas for a blog post. With the RSS reader you avoid the site surfing - the posts comes to you.

2. Interview people pertinent to your topic. I have found that people are very willing to do interviews for a blog. Send them 8-10 questions via e-mail. When they send back their responses, the post is practically written for you.

3.   Invite people to be guest bloggers; perhaps writing one post per month.

4. Try writing reviews of books that relate to your subject area. These are generally easier to write than other types of posts.

5. Do a "Links of the Day" type of post. This is basically a list of 4-5 sites that you find really interesting and think your readers might, too. You can write a one sentence annotation of each link to give them an idea of what they will find when they click on it.

6. Do a "5 things . . ." type of post. This is a post that has a title like "5 Things You Should Always Do when [fill in the blank]." It is just a simple bulleted list. People tend to like these because they are useful and easy to read.

7. Go to YouTube and add a video that highlights what you are talking about. The maxim that a picture is worth a thousand words definitely applies in blogging.

8. If you blog about things that are topical or in the news, set up a Google alert based on a useful you did about that topic. Then Google will automatically rerun the search and e-mail you the results based on a frequency you specify. You can get multiple posts by continuing to update a story with the new information you get from the alerts.

9. Monitor your topic or story on Twitter. You will often find new twists to a story, people you can interview or links to sites that provide great information you can incorporate into your posts.

An editorial calendar also helps you synchronize your blog content with your book outline, to ensure that you are representing all of the material in your book. This is important since you will want to use your blog metrics to identify the most viable content and you do not want to leave any material untested.

Map Blog Posts to Book Outline with Tags

Once you have structured your blog to resemble your book and established your editorial calendar, the next step is adding content in a consistent, cohesive manner. In a certain sense, you can develop your style as a writer beginning with the manner in which you customize your blog content for presentation in a book. Taking content from blog posts and turning it into a readable manuscript can be a challenging task, especially when you have a large inventory of blog posts from which to draw. There are two tools, the *book outline* and *post sequencing*, that can help you organize your posts into a manuscript in a logical manner, right from the start, without massive rewriting.

Post Tagging Overview

First, use your manuscript outline as a tool for cataloging your posts. An outline is always a good writing practice to employ anyway, but now it can also help you organize your blog posts. Here is how it works. First, create a set of labels that identify where, in your book outline, the content from each blog post will go. Provide a unique label for each element of your book outline. Next, apply one or more of these labels as tags to each blog post you write. (Recall from Chapter Two that this is done using the tagging feature of your blogging software.) You may have more than one label per post simply because the content of the post may be appropriate for multiple places in your book outline. This process is shown schematically in figure 5-1 below.

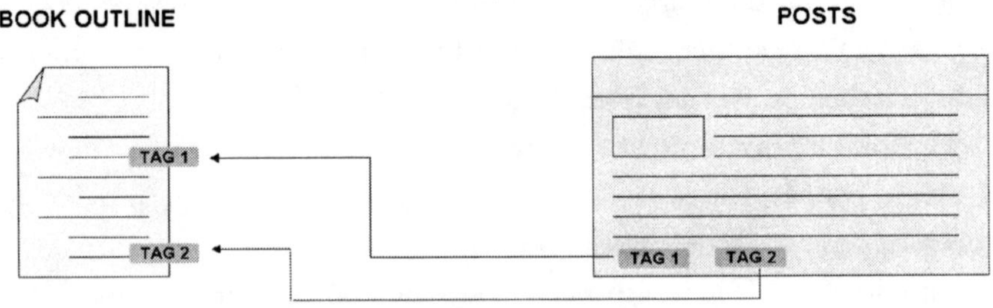

1. **Create a book outline with the topmost level corresponding to the blog categories.**
2. **Use post tags that match up to keywords and phrases in the lower levels of the book outline.**
3. **Organize blook content by filtering on these tags.**

Figure 6-1 Use tags to organize blog content

Finally, when you are ready to pull blog content into your book outline, go to the dashboard of your blogging software and filter your posts by entering each tag as a search keyword. Your blogging software will automatically pull up the appropriate content so you can flesh out each part of your book outline.

Post Tagging and Sequencing Strategies

You have seen that tags are essential to indicate the specific intended location of a post's content within the manuscript outline. One approach to doing this is to create an outline with a hierarchical numbering scheme and then use the sequence numbers from the outline as your tags.

For example, let's say you are writing a book about dogs. In your book outline, "Dog Nutrition" occupies all of Chapter 3. Within this chapter, the third section discusses dog treats, and the fourth subsection talks about organic dog treats. If you had a post about the different types of organic dog treats archived in the blog category "Dog Nutrition" it might be tagged with a single label such as "organic-dogfood-3-3-4." The tag reminds you that this is about organic dog treats and the sequence numbers tell you where in the book outline the post belongs. The sequence numbers are as long as the number of levels in the book outline. Such sequence tagging allows you to later use the post search tools of your blog to find and organize posts corresponding to each part of your outline.

Of course, book outlines are subject to change. Chapters can be added, inserted or deleted and this can cause problems with post sequencing based on outline numbering. An alternative approach might be to code tags with names that correspond to the outline labels. That way, if the outline changes, the tags on your blog posts are still valid. Again, using our dog manuscript outline above, let's say your organic dog food treat was about chicken flavored tofu. Using this alternative scheme, you might code the post with multiple tags corresponding to the book outline levels such as "nutrition, organic, treats, chicken tofu." Here the tags are arranged in the descending order of the outline. If there are multiple posts about chicken flavored tofu treats for your dog, you can assign a sequence number as the final tag, or find a text label that distinguishes them further.

The advantage of this approach to tagging is that should you decide to move "dog nutrition" to some other part of the book outline, your post tagging sequences still remain valid. If you make dog nutrition part of a chapter on dog health, you can simply add a tag "dog health" to the head of all your tag lists for dog nutrition.

Creating a book outline using one of the post sequencing techniques described above greatly simplifies the task of organizing your blog content into a manuscript. Good organization is only the first step. Later in this chapter, other editorial processes are identified which must be applied to get a manuscript that doesn't feel chopped up.

Decide Which Posts to Use

As you start to post, you will want to use blog statistics to rank content and track your word count so that you know when you have a book equivalent. A good rule of thumb for a book equivalent is 50,000 - 75,000 words. You should also track the word count by category. Remember that your categories are acting as surrogates for chapters. You want to be sure your content is relatively balanced as you go so you do not wind up with too much or too little content in each chapter.

There are several ways to rank content. Here are a few examples.

- **Pageviews.** This simple count is a good indicator of the level of overall interest in a particular post.

- **Comments.** Comments represent feedback from your readership. A post with a high number of comments is a good indicator of blook-worthy content.

- **Longevity.** This metric is computed as follows: Calculate the number of days between the original post and the last day for which there are page views. Divide this quantity by the age of the post (number of days since the original post). Longevity is useful to find topics that might be evergreen. The closer the longevity is to 1.0, the more durable the content.

- **Concentration.** This is the age of the post (days since the original post) divided by the number of days for which there are page views. Some posts may see all their activity concentrated in a few days (e.g., posts related to news stories) and thus, may not be as "durable" as a post that continues to receive page views day after day. The higher the concentration, the more likely the post has a value that diminishes with time.

- **Density.** Density is the number of page views for the post divided by the overall page views for the blog. This shows the contribution of the post to overall blog activity. The higher the density, the more valuable the content.

These metrics will change over time. It is probably a good idea to recalculate them once a month after you start blogging. The metrics can be organized into a spreadsheet which you can use to help sort posts by the value of each type of metric.

Edit Your Posts into a Manuscript

Once you have collected the posts you want to use in your manuscript and organized them to fit within your book outline, the next step is editing them into a coherent, cohesive whole. Below are some simple guidelines that will help you streamline this process.

Make the tone uniform. Blog posts often have a tone that may be too informal or too editorial for a book. Form some simple rules around style and tone that can be a guide for editing your blog post content. Such rules may relate to the use (or avoidance) of certain vocabulary, sentence length and reading level.

Keep the tense consistent. Blog posts are often written in the first person singular. This is natural since a blog typically bears the personality of its owner. But this may not work well in your manuscript. Be sure to adopt the appropriate voice across all of the posts you plan to use in your manuscript.

Eliminate time based references. Blog posts often reference topical information in a time specific way. For instance, phrases like "last Monday" or "the recent political summit" may be fine in the context of your blog, but may not be appropriate for your book. Be sure to eliminate or modify such time based references from your blog to be consistent with the time base of your manuscript.

Quote your sources and references. Blog posts are often full of links to other sites, videos or previous blog posts. When you bring blog post material into your book, these links lose their entire context. Since readers won't be able to click through to get that context, you will need to provide the site name and

URL, as well as some background about the content it references. This can be done either directly within the text or as a bibliographic reference or end note.

Decide which visual assets to keep. You may have incorporated illustrations, photos or charts in your blog posts that you will not be able to use as is in your manuscript; at least not without acquiring permissions to use them. Keep a list of the visual assets you would like keep as part of your manuscript. These can serve as placeholders for visual material you want to create or acquire later for your book.

Read through your manuscript carefully to ensure that you delete specific mention of those visual assets you do not want to retain in your manuscript. This may entail rewriting or expanding the text that referred to those assets.

Track and Collect Your References

An important part of many non-fiction works is citing references in the footnotes or endnotes of the book. There are three strategies you can use for this task:

- Using the links in context within the blog posts you incorporate into your book
- Storing links on a social bookmarking site like *del.icio.us*
- Using your browser's favorites list

Use In-context Links for References

The links you use in your blog posts that point to other sites with relevant information are in essence reference citations. When you convert a blog post into text for your book, you can insert a footnote or endnote where the link was that can serve as your reference. (You may need to follow the link from your blog to remind yourself what the source is and gather additional information for your citation.) The position of your blog post within the book outline determines the position of the footnote or endnote. Turning post links into citations will certainly ease the process of annotating your work.

However, there will no doubt be circumstances where you have additional online information not incorporated into your blog. For this purpose, you can use a social bookmarking site or your browser's *favorites list* to remember your link. Let us look at the social bookmarking strategy first.

Bookmark Your References

Bookmarking sites provide a good way to capture online resources. These sites allow you to share the URL of a website you find interesting. As part of the process of bookmarking, you provide a brief description of the site and a set of tags that you believe characterize the content of the site. What makes this valuable is the tagging process. Collectively, these tags help classify the site from the visitor's perspective rather than that of the site owner.

This feature makes bookmarked sites a great research tool in and of themselves. You can perform searches to find sites that others have tagged with the keywords or phrases you are searching on.

Bookmarks can be public or private. It is probably a good idea to keep the bookmarks you have acquired in the development of your manuscript private until your book has been published. For the sites you will use as citations in your book, you should apply the same tagging you are using to map your blog posts to your book outline. This will allow you to more precisely position the reference in your work.

When it comes time to add footnotes and endnotes to your book, it is an easy matter to copy your bookmarks to your manuscript. However, your bookmarks should be labeled in a way that correlates to their position within the book outline.

Saving Your References in Your Favorites List

An easy way to save reference links is in the *favorites folder* that is part of your browser software. Create one top level folder that has the title of your book and organize a set of subfolders by chapter. The advantage to this method is ease of setup. The disadvantage is that it is more difficult to include positioning information for the link below the chapter level.

Summary

In this chapter, we examined the different strategies used to go from blog to (non-fiction) book and reviewed examples for different blook motifs. CAUTION: Not every blog translates well into a book. Each medium has its own aesthetics and moving from blog to print may require significant editing or rewriting of content.

The most important consideration in going from blog to book is: Do you have an audience that will follow you into print? Once you have answered this in the affirmative, you can design your blog posts to make the job of editing content into book form easier.

6

Blog Your Novel

Many authors are discovering that the blogosphere is a good place to showcase their works of fiction and build a community of devoted readers. Consider the case of Scott Sigler. Scott writes science-fiction horror novels, described by a fan as a "steel-tipped boot on your throat, speed-metal fiction."

Snubbed by agents and publishers for years, Scott decided to try a different approach. He decided to use podcasting. As Scott recounted in an interview with Future Perfect Publishing:[19]

"I discovered podcasting in February 2005. I immediately started looking for podcast novels, because the technology reminded me of radio plays of the 40s and 50s, serialized audio fiction. When I couldn't find any novels, I realized it was because no one had done it yet. *EarthCore* was set to be published in 2002 by AOL/TimeWarner, but they scrapped the imprint a month or so before my book was printed. So I had a finished novel, edited by a major publishing house, just sitting there. I learned how to podcast and got the thing up as fast as I could, knowing there would be benefit to first-mover status."

He recorded *EarthCore*, in 2005 in 22 audio episodes (roughly 45 minutes each) that subscribers downloaded for free. His audience quickly grew to 5,000 listeners; and when he finished his second novel, *Ancestor*, it acquired 30,000 listeners. *The Rookie*, his current novel which is available for download now, has a similar sized audience. Initially, he recorded these "podcasts" of his works in a walk-in closet in his San Francisco home; it was the only space that had the sound deadening material he needed to achieve a quality recording. He provided the voices for all of his characters.

Once he made publishers aware of the size of his audience and their enthusiasm for his work, he had no trouble attracting a Canadian publisher,

Dragon Moon Press, which published *EarthCore* and *Ancestor*. Today, he continues to pilot his works in podcast format and his titles are being published by Crown Books.

Scott summarized his advice to authors about the wisdom of this approach to publishing:[20]

"At the end of the day, publishers spend a load of money to produce, distribute and market books. If you can prove to them that you have an existing audience, they are more likely to take a chance on you."

Different Ways to Blog Your Novel

Fictions writers have experimented with a number of different blogging motifs to build their readership. These are grouped into the following categories:

- Excerpts
- Full story online
- Podiobook
- Blog where the author is the story

Each motif involves a greater or lesser degree of exposure of the material to the audience and is described in the sections below.

Excerpts

Excerpts represents the most common method used by writers who blog their work. Excerpt can involve sample chapters, back story and / or progress notes from the author. Cherie Priest is an example of an author who used this approach to build her audience.

Cherie Priest (born 30 July 1975) is an American novelist who is best known for her debut novel *Four and Twenty Blackbirds*, which was published in 2003. In addition to her novels, Ms. Priest publishes two online blogs: one personal (called *Heretic Spire – A Damn Lie* at http://cmpriest.livejournal.com), one professional (called *Fathom* at http://www.cheriepriest.com), and is at the head of the growing presence of authors online, being in contact with many others via their blogs. It is partially due to this online "networking" that her first novel was such a cult success, having been promoted by many authors to their readers.

The 2005 edition of *Four and Twenty Blackbirds*, is an example of the emerging genre of blog fiction, because a substantial part of the work was serialized and promoted on her blog at LiveJournal. It was through this serialization that she built a readership for her work from both fans and industry professionals. It is common for Priest to post teasers of work in progress, or whole chapters of finished work, on her blog to promote her work.

Excerpts don't always have to be in the form of text. A different sort of blog novel project is a graphic novel (also known as *manga*) being developed by Beckett Gladney and Deborah Ridpath Ohi. The project originated after Ms. Ridpath Ohi, who had written some young adult novels that took place in a town called Curiosity, decided to turn these into graphic novels instead. She recruited Ms. Gladney to create the artwork. Their blog, named *Curiosity* (http://www.debbieohi.com/milo), features sketches, plot synopsis, writing samples, and a running commentary about the novel's progress as well as research about the comic / graphic novel industry.

The advantage of this blog-to-book approach is that it doesn't expose the audience to all of the content. The samples whet readers' appetites and the pre-publication exposure of some parts of the novel make fans feel closer to the author and have an inside view to the book's development process.

Full Story Online

An extension of the excerpt strategy is to provide all of the book's contents on the blog. Some authors may view this as risky for two reasons. First, the material might be copied; second, book publishers might not be interested in a work that has already been shown online. Plagiarism is always a concern, but can be mitigated to some degree by serialization. And, building a quantifiable fan base online is one of the best ways to get a publisher or agent interested in your work.

An example of this approach to the blog novel can be found in the writings of Declan Burke, an Irish crime story writer who is successful both online and offline. His current crime novel, *Gonzo Noir*, can be found at the book's website at http://agonzonoir.blogspot.com. His second novel, *The Big O*, has recently been published by Harcourt in the United States.

Podiobook

Humanity never tires of hearing a good story. In ancient times, stories were told around a roaring campfire. The oral tradition evolved and continues even after the written word had become the dominant way to retain cultural knowledge. Radio, and now podcasts, are its modern incarnation.

The podcast novel is finding its place in the publishing world as a way for independent authors to build an audience when publishers won't bite. Some authors have achieved remarkable success telling their stories in the "podiobook" format.   J.C. Hutchins is a prime example. He built a highly active Internet community around his work without ever publishing in print form. He has finally relented and decided to publish one of his three novels, *7th Son: Descent* in 2009.

Mr. Hutchins described the evolution of his writing and podcasting in an interview with *Future Perfect Publishing*.[21]

"From 2002 to 2004, I wrote what we now know as the "7th Son trilogy" as one long manuscript. The complete story - nearly 1,300 pages in length - was far longer than any publisher would purchase and release from a first-time novelist. Egotistically, I ignored this and spent 2005 querying literary agents. I received deserved universal rejections from the industry. The project I'd spent two years of my life writing (and breathing) was dead on arrival. It was disheartening.

"During 2005, I was listening to podcasts and discovered the serialized "podcast novel" works of Scott Sigler, Tee Morris, Mark Jeffrey, Jack Mangan and others, and realized that if I couldn't sell *7th Son*, I could at the very least share it. In early 2006, I chopped my monster manuscript into thirds (act one became Book One: Descent, etc.) and began releasing it as a podcast. More than two years, and more than 40,000 listeners and nearly 2 million downloads later, I now have a print deal for that first novel in the *7th Son* series. It will be released next Fall [2009] by St. Martin's Press.

"And yes, I have another novel that will be released in Summer 2009, also by St. Martin's. This for-hire project, called *Personal Effects: Dark Art*, is an ambitious novel-meets-Alternate Reality Game supernatural thriller that will break more than a few rules in the way readers perceive and experience prose fiction. This deal also hailed directly from the success of the 7th Son podcast. St. Martin's Press associate editor David Moldawer facilitated both deals.

"How do I think my audience will respond to these two print releases next year? I think they're going to love it. I've received thousands of emails from fans during the past two-and-a-half years as a podcaster, and a great many of them specifically mention how excited they are to know that these books will be published, and how they'll purchase copies for themselves and friends. I'm humbled by this, as I believe they, the fans, are the No. 1 reason for any success I've experienced as an author."

So what is a podiobook? A podiobook (or podcast novel) is a term coined by Evo Terra to describe serialized audio books which are made available in podcast format. Innovative authors are evolving podcast novels by adding more production values than simple voice recordings. In some sense, it is following the creative arc of old time radio drama. Some of these enhancements include:

- Guest voices on a podcast
- Sound effects
- Music to heighten the emotional impact
- Building community with the podcast audience by posting listener feedback on a blog associated with the podcast

All of these add emotional impact and help the reader better imagine the story. Creating a podcast novel takes work, however. A lot more work than writing a blog. Some of the considerations include:

- Format, i.e., whether single or multiple voices, other production values, how long each episode should be, etc.

- Recording equipment and editing software. The tools you use will depend on the requirements of your podcast as well as your comfort level with technology; don't underestimate the learning curve

- Time investment. Episodes can easily take upwards of 8 hours to fully produce and distribute; longer if you are adding voices, sound effects and music

- Costs for hosting, storage and bandwidth usage (the quantity of data being downloaded from your site)
- Tracking downloads and getting / responding to feedback from your audience

J.C. Hutchins provides an informative description of the process he used for podcasting each episode of *7th Son*:

"Creating a typical podcast episode for a serialized audiobook such as mine involves recording what I call the "core content" (the chapter that will be released in that weekly episode), editing out all the reading flubs, writing and recording timely announcements that preclude and conclude the core content, adding promotional recordings for other podcasts, mixing the entire production down into an episode, uploading it to a Web server, and then activating the content in my podcast feed.

"I won't bore your readers with the minutiae of the things I had to learn in those early days, but they involved learning what affordable recording gear to purchase (in 2006, I spent around $100 for the microphone and mixer that I still use), using an audio editing program (I use the free Garageband program for the Macintosh; there are free programs for other computer platforms, as well), understanding the fundamentals of what powers a podcast (RSS and XML technologies), and how to build and manage a website. It sounds daunting, but nearly all of this stuff was easy to grok [understand], once I realized that I didn't have to be a "master" of all of these things at once. Like writing a novel, I baby-stepped my way through learning these things, and only after I was confident that I knew the basics did I launch my podcast.

"The greatest revelation I made about podcasting my fiction was that it can be a colossal time suck. I'm a solid performer of my work, but I'm a terrible reader. Recording a typical 45-minute episode takes around 90 minutes for me, and another three hours to edit it. Even more time is required to write and record the timely announcements. The mixdown of an episode can take as long as 30 minutes. Even more time is taken uploading the final audio file to the Web, and activating it for people to download.

"The technology is relatively easy to master, but the time investment can be enormous."[22]

There are many good references to help you get started. One of the best is *Podcasting Bible* by Steve Mack and Mark Ratcliffe. The authors provide a comprehensive overview of the subject and take you through the four stages of a podcast:

- Planning,
- Recording and editing
- Encoding
- Distribution

One of the things you will need to be especially aware of is that success has its costs. Generally, podcast distribution services charge for storage and throughput. Throughput can be expensive if thousands of fans start downloading your serialized story podcasts. Be sure to check the terms of your podcast hosting service or distribution network and calculate what a popular podcast might wind up costing you.

Blogs Where the Author is the Story

Often times it is a blog's author who is the real story. The content of the blog itself may not become a book, but rather serves as the basis for creating something different but related. It is more like bait that attracts the attention of publishers or television and film producers. We offer for consideration two examples of "blog as bait:" *Belle du Jour* and the blogs of Diablo Cody.

Belle de Jour is (supposedly) the blog of a high-class London call girl, Belle, whose identity is a closely guarded secret. (The name was taken from the 1967 movie which starred Catherine Deneuve playing a prostitute named Séverine Serizy.) The secrecy around Belle's true identity makes the story that much more interesting. The Times Online reported on rumors[23] that had surfaced in a blog, *Belle de Hypothesis*, that Belle is actually the creation of writer Lisa Hilton and a "coterie of young women who saw it as an appropriate vehicle to vent their frustrations with various aspects of their personal and professional lives."[24] Ms. Hilton is an Oxford educated author living in the U.S. A self professed sexual adventuress, she has written a very candid article exposing her own sexual exploits.

Sixteen months after starting the diary, Belle not only won herself a six-figure book deal (*The Intimate Adventures of a London Call Girl* published in the

U.K. by Phoenix and *Belle de Jour: Diary of an Unlikely Call Girl* published in the U.S. by Grand Central Publishing), but her story has also been adapted for television. The television show is *The Secret Diary of a London Call Girl* and she is being played by Billie Piper on BBC's Channel 4. The book deal was carefully arranged so that the true name of *Belle de Jour's* author would not be revealed.

The writing is true diary style. Belle is detailed, frank and practical in her descriptions of her work and her clients. According to the author of *Belle de Hypothesis*, the earlier works of Lisa Hilton lend credence to rumors that she is the true Belle. Her book Athenais: The Life of Louis XIV Mistress-the Real Queen of France chronicles the life of Athenais de Montespan, the favorite mistress of the Sun King and documented "the incredible adventures of a woman who lived brazenly." In this case, the mystery about the author of *Belle du Jour* is as intriguing as the stories found in its posts.

Blog to book stories can offer strange twists, but none is as unusual as that of Diablo Cody. Diablo Cody, a pen name for Brook Busey-Hunt, graduated with a degree in media studies from the University of Iowa and, according to an article in Wikipedia,[25] started her career quietly enough proofreading ad copy for Minneapolis radio stations. Her first blog was Darling Girl, which detailed her daily experiences and interactions. On a whim, she took up stripping and later switched to being a phone sex operator. Her blogging would, like her career, later become a notch more risqué.

At the age of 24, Cody published the memoir *Candy Girl: A Year in The Life of an Unlikely Stripper.* Prior to publication, Cody's blog writing had attracted the attention of Mason Novick (*Red Eye*) who thought she had a fresh voice and wondered if she would consider writing a movie. As related in a *Seattle Times* article,[26] he called her and suggested she write a screenplay. Cody, flattered by Novick's confidence in her, obliged and wrote *Juno,* the story of a pregnant teen, who with the support of her loving but eccentric family, decides to have the baby and give it to an infertile couple. Jason Reitman (*Thank you for Smoking*) directed the film. Now she is head writer for Steven Spielberg's new TV series *The United States of Tara,* she has more movies in the works, and recently the Hollywood Film Festival gave her the Hollywood Breakthrough Screenwriter of the Year Award. (Her breathless ascent to Hollywood writer 'Nirvana' is chronicled in a *Wired* article, *Diablo Cody's Tips for Blogging Your Way to Hollywood Success.*)[27]

Cody's writing certainly provokes reactions on both sides of the spectrum. But as the *LA Times* noted, her voice is authentic and refreshing:[28]

"In a town that shells out millions of dollars for screenplays so practiced that they read as though the human element has all but been squelched, hers is an authentic voice, alternately sardonic, wide-eyed, hilarious and sad.

"'I've always gotten a large ration of negative reactions to positive in my writing,' she says."For some reason, it tends to provoke reactions on the extreme ends of the spectrum. I hate the idea that I'm some sort of self-invented Gatsby-type figure who clawed her way to the top. I have done nothing of the sort. I'm Forrest Gump. I feel like I'm superimposed in all these scenarios. I don't know what the hell I'm doing here.' "

Cody is certainly a refreshing conundrum, an unexpected mishmash and a self-declared "radical feminist" who's routinely receives angry e-mails from readers who believe that's she a female chauvinist, complicit with the porn industry. Her memoir *Candy Girl* is certainly not for the fainthearted, full of the up-close-and-personal details of what it's like to strip and entertain depraved customers. Her book combines prurience with a wacky sense of humor and Midwestern "do-it-yourselfness"; it landed her a David Letterman one-and-only "Book Club 2006 pick" and a jaunty appearance on the show, where she declared herself the "Margaret Mead of sex."

Just as publishers are beginning to explore the blogosphere for commercial grade writing talent, look for Hollywood to follow suit. But what is compelling and interesting about Diablo Cody's work is not that she went from blog to book or from blog to script; but rather that she went from life to both of the above.

Selecting a Blog Novel Strategy

The strategy you choose to blog your novel depends on several factors, including:

- Where you are in the development of your work
- The type of story you are telling
- How engaged you want to be with your audience
- Time investment you are willing to make

- Your publishing goals

Development stage. If you are in the early stages of your book's development, you may wish only share general aspects of the work. This might include some information about the characters, some of their back story and the overall plot line. You might even include a sample chapter. An excerpt strategy would be most appropriate; it allows you to give your readers a taste of what is coming and the opportunity for them to give some useful feedback. If your work is completed, you might want to share the full story in a serialized form, either text or podcast.

Type of story. Stories with a large amount of action and dialogue might do better in a podcast format. Fiction that is more narrative or whose plot is slower moving might be better suited to text.

Audience engagement. The podiobook provides a more emotional engagement with your readers, especially if you are doing all the voices.

Time investment. As we have seen from the experience of Scott Sigler and J.C. Hutchins, podiobooks can require a much greater investment of time to create than creating a blog post. (In the case of both of these authors, they maintain an active blog in addition to their podcasting.)

Publishing goals. The goals you establish for your work play an important role in determining how you want to connect your readers with your book online. Are you trying to find a publisher or agent, or are you planning to self-publish your work? Many authors are fearful that if they share their work online, publishers will reject it. However, it is important to remember that what interests publishers is the size of your audience and the desire of those readers for your work. Another consideration is whether the first work you develop is intended to establish an audience, and use that to land a publisher for your follow-on work. This is the strategy used by Declan Burke.

Summary

In Chapter 3 we discussed how to use blogs to write non-fiction titles. In this chapter, we examined the growing popularity of the blog novel and have looked at examples of four different strategies for creating a blog novel. These include:

- Excerpts
- Full story online
- Podiobook
- Blog where the author is the story

You should carefully evaluate the advantages and disadvantages of each strategy to determine which approach works best for you. In the next chapter, we will look at ways to measure your readership and the popularity of your content. These metrics can form the basis for a book pitch that will have strong appeal for publishers and agents.

7
Pitch Your Book with Metrics

Over the years, authors have received much well meaning advice about how to prepare book proposals. This usually includes providing a compelling summary of the book, the intended audience, competing titles and the reasons why the author's book would stand out against these other titles.

The writer can probably develop a good summary, but when it comes to audience and competition, many authors draw a blank. First of all, they have no pool of actual readers from which to draw conclusions. Second, they have no idea about how readers might react to the content and style of their writing. With a typical manuscript, almost no one sees it before it "goes live."

When is Your Blog a Book?

Authors who blog may have the intention to create a book from their efforts or may be prodded to either by their audience or by a publisher who spots an opportunity in their blogging success. If you have been blogging regularly for some period of time, it is easy to lose track of the content you have created. Posts and comments accumulate, but as time passes, they slip into the archives.

So how can you tell when it is time to consider turning your blog into a book?

Here are some potential factors to consider. First, have you established an engaged and loyal readership? Second, how much content do you have and how well organized is it? And third, which content is suitable for publication?

The answer to the first question can be found in the myriad of traffic statistics available for web sites and blogs which we discuss below. For example, unique visitors, number of feed subscribers (assuming you have enabled RSS feeds), average number of page views per month, downloads, etc. A sample of the broad scope of statistics you can collect for your blog can be found by taking the tour at *Clicky* (www.getclicky.com), just one of a multitude of web analytics service providers.

The second question can be answered by examining the total word count for all your posts and comments. Take this number and divide it by the typical word count in an average size book, say 75,000 to 90,000 words. What you come up with is the number of book equivalents. Since not all content may be appropriate for a single book, more than one book equivalent may be necessary to produce a coherent title. The strength of the content organization can be determined in part by the categories you have used. Categories can, if chosen properly, mirror the chapters in a book or at least major topic areas. If there is a good balance of content across relevant categories, the material is off to a good start.

Knowing what posts are most popular and evoke the most response is a good clue as to what content will most likely do well in a book. If you provide content for download, knowing what material gets downloaded most often is also a good indicator for inclusion in a title. Another indicator is which posts get bookmarked on social bookmarking sites such as *Digg*, *Reddit* and *del.icio.us*.

Basic Metrics for Authors

The first step in understanding your audience is to get familiar with basic blog metrics that:

- Quantify the content you (and your readers) have produced
- Measure the traffic to your blog
- Characterize the behavior and engagement of your readers
- Summarize the impact your blog has made

In this section, we describe some of the basic metrics commonly provided by most blogging platforms or tracking services. Later in this chapter we will focus on more advanced metrics that will help you select the most compelling blog content for use in your book.

Content

You may well ask why it is necessary to measure your output. Don't you already know how much content you are producing?   The answer is "yes" when you first start out. But as time goes on and you write more posts, those posts find their way into your archives. As you create additional items for download, it is easy to lose track of just how much content you have available.

The more content you create on a blog, the more likely, over time, you are to attract and sustain a readership. It is, then, worth having some indication of just what is available.

Fortunately, many of the popular blogging platforms simplify this task by making the data available for free. Here are some useful numbers to start with:

- Number of pages
- Number of categories
- Number of posts
- Number of words in posts
- Number of comments
- Number of words in comments

From these raw content metrics, you can gain a clear indication of what you have to offer readers in quantity. Tracking over time with the other metrics discussed below helps determine whether the value of this content is increasing or decreasing from the point of view of your readers. Table 6-1, *Useful Derivative Content Metrics*, provides additional information derived from the raw content metrics and gives you a way to interpret this data.

Once you have accumulated a large body of content and developed an audience for it, you may want to consider repurposing that content into a book. An established blog audience is a great place to start marketing a book. Many bloggers are finding this an effective strategy for heightening their expertise and their blogging profile. But how do you know when it is time to turn your blog into a book? This is where the *book equivalent* comes in. Take the total word count of your posts, divide it by the number of words in a typical book for your topic area (say 75,000 to 90,000 words), and you have the number of book equivalents in your blog. You probably need to have something more than one *book equivalent* since not all content may translate easily into book format.

If you decide from the start that your goal is to turn the content of your blog into a book, take great care in naming categories and balancing the content among them. The categories are in some sense the "chapters" of your book and the posts within them will be each chapter's content.

Metric	Derivation	Interpretation
# total words	# words in posts + # words in comments + # words in pages	Raw overall word count
# book equivalents	# total words / 90,000	Useful analogy to how many books of information the site contains
Average post length	# words in posts / # posts	Approx. quantity of information delivered per post
Average posts per month	# posts / # months	Posting frequency and trend over time
Average comments per post	# comments / # posts	Rough measure of audience engagement
Category – post distribution	Graph of # posts per category	Shows where your topic focus is and how it is evolving over time
Category – comment distribution	Graph of # comments per category	Shows the categories that evoke the most response from your readers and how it is evolving over time
Author load	# posts / # authors	Shows how much each author is contributing (if yours is a blog with guest authors)

Table 5 -1 Useful Derivative Content Metrics

Traffic

Traffic[1] measures are perhaps the most exciting type of metrics because they provide an indication of how many people are coming to your blog and what they are doing while they are there. These data are collectively known as *web analytics*. Some of the more common traffic data from an analytics tool include:

- Hits
- Visits
- Unique visitors
- Page views
- Referrals
- Search strings
- Entry pages
- Exit page
- Feed subscriptions
- Feed subscribers
- Overall blog readership

Hits. A hit is logged when a file is delivered by your web server to someone's browser. Every page on your blog consists of one or more files. There is the HTML file and possibly image files, Flash files, and advertisements. Thus, when someone visits one of your pages, your server is likely to register multiple hits. Hits are a rough, but not very useful, indicator of traffic to your blog site.

Visits. A visit consists of all the pages viewed by an individual when they come to your blog site. The visit begins when the person first comes to your site and ends when they exit the site. Visits provide a more finely tuned measure of traffic to your blog, but are still relatively coarse.

Pageviews. Pageviews, unlike hits, count all the files associated with a page as one package. Pageviews tell you the extent to which your content is being consumed (viewed) and which pages are most popular.

Unique visitors. A unique visitor is a single individual making a visit to the site. Each individual visiting your blog site is only counted once. This is a truer measure of the audience you are reaching than either visits or hits. Note that unique visitors do not generally include people who may be reading your blog posts via an RSS feed. How to count those individuals is discussed below.

Referrals. A referral is a link from a web page to one of the pages on your blog. Referrals are set up when a website or blog links to you. Referrals also come when someone clicks on a link in a *search results page(SRP)* to get to your blog. Referrals are useful because they indicate where traffic is coming from and where to focus your blog marketing efforts.

Search Strings. These are the keywords and phrases that people type into search engines to find your blog. They are valuable because they indicate what your visitors are interested in and provide potential keywords to use on your blog.

Entry pages. These are the pages where visitors enter your blog. For example, this could be the home page of the blog where your most current posts reside, or a page containing a post from your blog archives.

Exit page. This is the last page a visitor views before leaving your blog.

Feed subscriptions. As discussed earlier, many individuals will choose to subscribe to your RSS feed and access your blog posts that way rather than surfing to your blog site. It is important to count these subscriptions to get a clear idea of just how many people are viewing your content. Feed metrics will depend on which feed services are being used. To help you gather this information, create a *Feedburner Pro* account and enable feed tracking. There is some thinking in the blogosphere that the numbers from feed services underestimate subscriber numbers, so to get a better estimate try multiplying your feed subscriber number by four.

Overall blog readership. Add your unique visitors and subscribers to measure your blog's readership. Most hosted blogging platforms will provide some basic traffic metrics for you, e.g., visitors, referrals, and page views. However, many of the web analytics services require you to put Javascript on your blog pages in order to gather their traffic data. Hosted platforms often block this for security reasons which may limit your ability to get the more detailed statistics we discussed above.

With these web analytics in hand, you are in a good position to know quite a bit about how many people are visiting your blog, where they are coming from, what keywords and phrases they use to find you, and what they do while they are visiting.

You will find it useful to track and trend this information on a weekly or monthly basis, but also correlate this data with events on your blog. For example, note particular posts that generated a lot of interest, traffic spikes caused when a popular blog referenced one of your posts, or referrals spawned when someone posted you on *Digg*. Keeping a journal of these events helps when you want to analyze and understand reader behavior.

Reader Engagement

Reader engagement includes several different components:

- Percent of readers creating comments
- How often readers comment on a post
- Length of reader comments
- Whether and how often readers bookmark your posts
- Whether and how often readers link to your posts in their blogs
- Whether and how often readers bookmark you on social networking sites[2]
- Whether and how often readers download items from your blog
- How much time readers spend on your blog during a visit

Approximate the first of these measurements by calculating the number of comments divided by the total number of unique visitors. This may not be exact because some visitors may comment more than once during a measurement period, but it will be close enough.

Measure the frequency of comments by dividing the total comments in a time frame by the number of days in that time frame.

The length of comments is already discussed above. You simply use the raw word count for all the comments and divide by the number of comments. Longer comments might indicate that your posts are effective at triggering a response from your readers.

Most blogging platforms will let you monitor the number of trackbacks for a given post. This will let you know how often your posts are being linked to from other blogs or sites. Generally this will only happen if someone liked what you said in your post. You can also use services such as *Google Alerts*,

Technorati, Blogpulse and *Yahoo! News,* to monitor inbound links, traffic, comments, and mentions of your blog.

Some bookmarking widgets actually notify you when someone has bookmarked your site. This is a handy way to figure out whether your audience thinks your post is worth letting others know about. Similar to trackbacks, this usually happens when someone is interested in what you had to say in your post.

Downloads may be more difficult to measure and could be dependent on the metric software you are using. If you provide downloads and can get this information, it is a very useful indicator that your readership is interested in these digital products, and may signal a higher level of trust in what you say.

Several metrics offerings allow you to track where individuals go on your site and how much time they spend. This indicates that they are exploring and is invaluable information as you fine-tune your site to visitor behavior patterns.

Impact

Impact here really means your blog's ranking in major search engines, especially the search engines that specialize in blogs (see Appendix D). Blog ranking is basically how you stack up relative to the other blogs in the blogosphere. Ranking for blogs is closely related to the ranking that search engines apply to websites to determine where sites appear in the list of search results. Below are some of the factors that may play a role in your blog's rankings. Remember that search engines vary in the way they calculate rank and the factors they use to make that calculation.

- **Link and citation influence.** This is a measure of how often your blog is cited by other bloggers or web-sites. It also takes into account the ranking of the blogs that link to your blog.

- **Longevity.** The length of time you have blogged is one of the factors that influences your blog's authority and ranking with the search engines.

- **Amount of content.** The content you produce is ultimately why people visit your blog. Your content may be downloaded, linked to, or shared widely across the Web. Content generates activity and, over time, that activity helps bring you higher rankings.

- **Audience engagement.** Engagement represents how many people visit your blog and perform some activity, e.g., leave comments on your posts, download a document, or click on a product link.

A good search engine to use for evaluating your blog ranking is *Technorati*.

Advanced Metrics for Content Selection

There are many ways to evaluate the suitability of blog content for your book. Good content has two important characteristics. First, it is popular, that is, people like to read it. Second, it is durable; it has continued readership beyond its initial posting. The metrics below provide a basic measurement of both of these characteristics and may be easily derived from the basic metrics discussed in the previous section.

- **Longevity.** This metric is computed as follows: Calculate the number of days between the original post and the last day for which there are page views. Divide this quantity by the age of the post (number of days since the original post). Longevity is useful to find topics that might be evergreen. The closer the longevity is to 1.0, the more durable the content.

- **Concentration.** This is the age of the post (days since the original post) divided by the number of days for which there are pages views. Some posts may see all their activity concentrated in a few days, e.g., posts related to news stories, and thus, may not be as "durable" as a post that continues to receive page views day after day. The higher the concentration, the more likely the post has a value that diminishes with time.

- **Contribution.** Contribution is the number of page views for the post divided by the overall page views for the blog. This shows the contribution of the post to overall blog activity. The higher the density, the more valuable the content.

Once these have been calculated for each post, you can rank your posts based on the values of these numbers. One way to make a decision about including content is to set a threshold for each of these measurements and only include content from those posts that exceed the threshold. This ranking provides one important consideration in the content selection process for your book, but it may not be the only one. Often you may need to include content that does not meet the threshold you set to preserve the consistency and coherence of your work.

The New Book Author Pitch

Baseball is one of the most analyzed games around. Alan Schwarz' bestseller, *The Numbers Game: Baseball's Lifelong Fascination with Statistics*, chronicles the evolution of the game's analytics and the public's semi-obsession with them. And, in *Moneyball* and *Baseball Between the Numbers*, readers learn there is a new interpretation of the decades old statistics led by Bill James. As a young boy, I was fascinated with baseball cards. The baseball card was the perfect, portable summary of a ball player's career, spelled out in neat rows of numbers.

As the publishing industry moves toward a more analytical driven model and authors take up the very measurable tool of blogging as a path to publishing, you can imagine a new book pitch that contains the following:

- A brief summary of the blog (soon-to-be book) concept
- A picture of the author with one or two sentence bio
- Blog traffic and behavior numbers
- Blog demographics

And if the font were small enough, it might all conveniently fit onto something the size of a baseball card. Suppose blogs had been available in Ernest Hemmingway's lifetime. Surely he would have blogged and used a pitch like the one contained on our imaginary card.

While we may not see such "author cards" anytime soon, the idea of incorporating blog statistics into a book proposal is certainly achievable and advisable. It tells the publisher that you have an audience that can be objectively measured and characterized. This type of metrics based book pitch also points the way to a marketing strategy. Your book could be marketed on blogs and sites that share a common theme.

Summary

In this chapter, we examined how you can effectively use blog metrics to help you quantify your readership and select the most compelling blog content for inclusion in your book. In the risk-averse world of book publishing, where editors are under unrelenting pressure to reduce risks and maximize profits, these metrics can form the basis for book proposals that get read and acted upon. Establishing an audience is important, but being able to provide objective data for the size and behavior of your readership is the key to a successful book pitch.

8
Go On a Blog Tour

Blogs represent a robust marketing platform, as well as being a venue for authors to develop their work and attract an audience. As we discussed in Chapter 1, blogs represent a new medium. Many blogs have readership that exceeds that of newspaper or even broadcast outlets. In recent years, many authors have taken advantage of this fact to use blogs as a way to market their work. Using blog search tools, authors can quickly find readers of other blogs with interests congruent with the content of their book. Instead of going on a physical book tour, authors create a "virtual" book tour on these blogs.

In this chapter, we will define what a blog tour is, discuss how to set up and manage a blog tour, as well as breakdown the costs associated with blog touring.

The Virtual Book Tour

A great example of how the new book marketing is Glenda Watson Hyatt, author of *I'll Do It Myself*. In her book, Ms. Hyatt shared her experiences living with cerebral palsy to motivate and inspire others to think about how they perceive their own situation and their own world around them. Amazingly, she does all this by typing with only her left thumb. One of the ways she is marketing her book is with a virtual blog tour. During the first 3 months of 2007, her tour included 40 blogs.

John Kremer, author of several book marketing titles, characterizes the virtual blog tour this way:

"A virtual blog tour is essentially a set of blog interviews or reviews. To set one up, you contact blogs related to your book as well as book blogs that review books and/or interview authors. Ask them if they'd like a review copy of your book and/or would like to interview you about your book. Tell them why your book or author would interest their audience.

Many blog interviews are done via e-mail where you answer a set of questions and email them back to the blog owner who posts the interview on his or her blog.

Your blog tour can start with sites that already link to your blog. You can also use blog search engines to find those *high authority, high traffic* sites that can give your book broad exposure. Blog tours are often overlooked by publishers and authors as a marketing tool. But once you consider that blogs now represent some of the largest media properties in terms of audience size, you can see the benefits of using this lost cost tactic. Some of the factors that make the blogosphere attractive as a marketing channel include:

- The blogosphere is big, with most topics & audiences represented
- Blogs tend to be audience and / or topic focused
- Topic / audience related blogs tend to link to each other, increasing the reach of your work to the right group of readers
- Blog linkages and traffic they bring are measurable

The concept of aggregating small niches to create a viable market is not new, especially in the fragmented micro-genre world of books. But the Internet has made it easier. Authors (or publishers) can use blog search tools to help them identify topic and audience compatible blogs for their tour. Using keyword discovery tools, like *SEOBook*. Popular words and phrases related to the title can be plugged into blog search engines to find the greatest number of likely candidates for a blog tour. The ranking and traffic stats (available on sites like *Alexa*) of each candidate blog can then be used as a way to filter out those whose impact may not be enough to warrant an interview. This can also lead to the discovery of new audiences that the author was not previously aware existed.

Blog Tours vs. Book Tours

Before delving deeper into the logistics and cost associated with blog tours, it is useful to compare them with conventional book tours. A typical book might take an author to a number of cities where he or she will make presentations, do book readings, participate in book signings and conduct interviews with the local media. Setting up and managing a book tour requires a great amount of planning, scheduling and coordination with involvement by publisher staff, the author, local media, event planners in the local venues and so on. There can also be considerable expense involved to cover travel, lodging and the local venues where an author might present. Who bears this cost depends on the agreement between publisher and author.

Blog touring, on the other hand, is much less time and cost intensive. The tasks associated with a blog tour can easily be handled by the author and the rewards, in terms of audience exposure and book sales can be much greater. The table below contrasts book touring and blog touring.

Blog Tour	Book Tour
virtual, no travel	actual, lots of travel
show on your book site, the blog(s) you will be a guest on	advertise in the local media of the cities where you will be appearing
light coordination	intensive coordination
exposure not limited by geography or time	exposure is usually limited by time & geography
sell via links to online booksellers or publisher site	sell at book signings and by promoting book at retail bookstores
inexpensive	expensive

Table 6.1 - Comparison of Book Tours and Blog Tours

Blog Touring Basics

The bestselling book *The Daring Book for Girls*, by Andrea Buchanan and Miriam Peskowitz was published by HarperCollins October, 2007. As part of the book launch publicity, the authors conducted a blog tour in October and November of that year. Some of the sites they visited included: *MothersTalk, Neatorama, Dr. Helen, DaddyDaze* and *HipMama*. This is another example demonstrating that many authors and some publishers are waking up to the use of blog tours as another publicity tool to help spread the buzz about pre-release or newly released titles.

But this is still relatively new marketing territory. Since I've been advising authors lately on the in's and out's of blog tours, I thought it might be useful to provide a short course in planning and executing a blog tour to kick off the new year.

A blog tour is pretty simple in concept. You find blogs whose readers might be interested in your title and you schedule virtual visits there. The blog tour process can be divided into four steps:

- Planning your tour
- Finding and contacting blog owners
- Conducting and tracking your tour
- Publicizing your tour
- Planning Your Tour

Planning Your Tour

The first order of business is to decide which blogs are the best to target the audience for your book. Start by creating a list of keywords that characterize your audience and the topics or story of your book. Then plug those keywords into various blog search engines – e.g. *Technorati* or *Ice Rocket* – to get a candidate list of blog sites for your tour. You can also use lists of high traffic blogs such as those found on *Forbes.com* or specialty sites such as *BlogFlux*.

One way to rank the blogs on your list is by their authority. Authority represents the number of sites linking to the blog within the last six months. Traffic statistics can sometimes be difficult to come by, and authority, which you can find on *Technorati* is a good proxy. As a general rule, the higher the authority, the higher the traffic. Sites with authority between one hundred and five hundred may be your best bet. They will likely have good traffic, but may still be small enough that you can make direct contact with the blog owner.

As part of the planning stage, create a blog appearance request e-mail. This is something you will send to the blog owner to request either an interview, a book review, or in some cases, to act as a guest blogger on the site for a period of time. Be sure to include the benefits their readers could gain from learning more about your book. At this stage, the tour request e-mail should be a template which you customize for each blog site contacted. A sample blog appearance request e-mail is included in Appendix E.

As part of the preparation gather:

- Author bio
- Recent photo
- Book cover image
- Testimonials if you have them
- A link to your blog or book website

Also, have several excerpts ready to provide blog owners for posting. (Note that some publishers will put limits on how much of your book they want to have excerpted prior to release). Blog owners who are conducting book reviews may want several chapters or an advance copy of the book. If the book has been listed on sites like Amazon prior to release, provide links as well as any other ordering information appropriate.

In the case of e-mail interviews, have a list of potential questions ready for blog owners. They are usually pressed for time and will appreciate the help.

Finding & Contacting Blog Owners

Once you have a list of good candidate blogs, create a spreadsheet where you can easily track them. Each row of the spreadsheet should contain:

- Blog name
- Blog site URL
- Blog owner name
- Blog owner e-mail address
- Field to track status, for example "contacted", "accepted", "declined", "tentative", and "completed"
- Appearance date
- Appearance type, that is, guest blogger, e-mail interview, book review
- Notes, for example, to record special requests from the blog owner like requesting a copy of the book in advance of the appearance

If you are using a spreadsheet program that allows multiple worksheets, e.g., *Microsoft Excel,* you can group all of the blogs associated with a specific audience segment onto one worksheet. This makes it easy to keep different audiences clearly separated. Another handy tracking mechanism is to create a summary worksheet that shows the total number of requests with status of "accept", "decline", or "tentative," as well as the overall response rate for your blog tour.

Now you are ready to send your blog appearance request e-mail. Some useful customizations for this e-mail request include:

- Blog name in the subject line

- Blog owner name in the salutation; if you don't know the blog owner's name, use something like "Dear <blog name> Owner"

- Mention the blog name and something specific about the blog

- Explain why you think your book is of interest to their readership

These simple customizations show the blog owner that you are interested in their readers and topic area. Be sure to respond quickly when a blog owner answers your request, and don't get discouraged if it takes awhile for some blog owners to respond. Many blog owners use *Google G-mail* accounts or web-based contact forms; they don't check these every day.

It is also a good idea to create an e-mail folder where you can keep all of your communications with blog owners. Depending on the number of blogs you contact, this can become voluminous over time.

Scheduling & Tracking Your Tour

Whenever possible, try to schedule your blog tour so that it straddles the release of your book and ties in with your other marketing efforts, such as a multi-city book tour or reviews in print publications. This will provide the maximum amount of buzz as your title comes to market.

Of course, the schedule is driven to some extent by the blog owners, but let them know what dates you are shooting for. Be sure to record the scheduled posting dates in your tracking spreadsheet. Also, try putting these on a calendar so you can see how concentrated or spread out your blog publicity efforts are becoming. With practice, you will become adept at scheduling your blog tour in the most efficacious way. Here are some simple guidelines for timing your tour:

Start with your release date and work both forward and backward from there. Begin researching and finalizing the blog sites for your tour, as well as pulling your request materials together about three months prior to release. Allow about two months for this part of the process. Allocate about a month after that for contacting and scheduling appearances. Conduct your tour from one month prior to release to one month after release. Then plan to monitor the traffic to the posts that were created for one month or so after your tour has been completed. This template blog tour schedule is summarized in Figure 6-1.

Figure 6-1 Sample blog tour schedule

After each appearance, it is a good idea to ask the blog owner to provide you with the number of visitors for the post where you and your book were featured. This data should run from the day of your appearance out to a couple of weeks thereafter. With this information, you can get an idea of the exposure that blog site generated by your appearance. Also be sure to note any favorable comments you received. You can record this information in your blog tour tracking spreadsheet.

Publicizing Your Tour

Finally, be sure to publicize your blog tour via press releases or by posting them on your blog or book website. This will make others aware of where your book will be featured.

Remember, there is nothing magic about a blog tour. It takes a lot of time and effort. Be prepared to spend several hours per blog site that accepts your blog tour request. But the buzz that you create is worth the effort. The great thing about an interview or review that appears on a blog is that it remains findable via search engines long after the title has gone to market. For more detailed information about setting up blog tours, check out Steve Weber's article in the PMA Independent.

So to all you courageous authors out there who want to leverage the viral powers of the Internet, good luck and happy touring!

Blog Tour Appearance Formats

There are numerous approaches to the way in which you make an appearance on one of blogs in the blog tour. We will focus on three blog tour formats here. These include:

- Guest blogger
- E-mail interview
- Book review

Guest blogger. In this approach, the blog owner gives the author guest blogging privileges. The blog owner introduces the author in a post and then the author writes a guest post about the book. The author then responds to comments that result from the post, up to some predetermined point in time.

E-mail interview. With the e-mail interview approach, the blog owner sends the author an e-mail with questions and the author responds to these in a reply e-mail. The blog owner then posts the interview along with a short author bio and a description of the book. For a predetermined period of time, the author prepares responses to any comments that result from the interview and sends these to the blog owner for posting.

Book review. In this approach, the author sends the blog owner chapters from the book or an advanced copy of the book. The blog owner then writes a book review and posts it with links to an author bio and book purchase sites. As with the e-mail interview approach, the author can write responses to any comments that result from the book review and e-mail these to the blog owner for posting.

Caveats about Blog Touring

While blog tours are simpler and more cost effective than conventional book tours, there are a number of things you should keep in mind when considering a blog tour for your book.

First, blog touring takes time. Setting up the tools for a blog tour like template e-mail, tracking spreadsheet and author information, will probably require 3-5 hours. You should allow 4-8 hours for researching blogs for each audience segment you want to address. To handle the contact and schedule coordination with blog owners, allow about 2 hours per blog site. And for your appearance and follow-up, budget 2-4 hours per site.

Second, not everyone will agree to participate in your blog tour. There is probably no such thing as a typical response rate at this point in time, but don't plan for anything greater than about a 20-25% response rate.

Finally, not all comments to your appearance will be favorable. But if you respond promptly and honestly to all comments, you are more likely to generate an overall positive response to your appearances.

An Interview with Steve Weber

In 2007, we interviewed Steve Weber, a well known book marketing expert, about virtual book tours as a marketing tool for authors and publishers. Steve, a former newspaper reporter, has been a full-time Internet bookseller since 2000, selling new, used and collectible books on sites such as *Amazon.com*, *Half.com*, and *eBay*. In 2005 he self-published his first book, *The Home-Based Bookstore*. The lessons he learned from promoting that book inspired *Plug Your Book: Online Book Marketing for Authors*. Originally from Charleston, W.Va., he resides in the Washington suburbs of northern Virginia. He spoke with us at *Future Perfect Publishing* about the in's and out's of virtual book tours.

FPP: What is a virtual book tour?

Steve: It's making a guest appearance on a blog that serves likely readers of your book. Sometimes it's called a "blog tour" or "guest blogging." So it's a good way of popping up in front of your target market, by going to a place where they already congregate. Blog tours are especially valuable for authors who can't travel or are uncomfortable with public speaking, and when touring is impractical because a book's readers are widely dispersed. Exactly how it's done depends on your preferences and the style of the blog. A plain-vanilla virtual book tour would be like newspaper editorials, but in the best case it's an interactive affair, and the author provokes a discussion among the blog readers. Typical blog tours include these elements:

- An excerpt displayed on each host blog in the days preceding the tour to publicize the tour appearance.

- A one-day appearance, beginning with a short essay on the topic of your book and then inviting discussion.

- Follow-up visits for the next four to seven days to answer questions and comments from blog readers.

FPP: How popular are virtual book tours with publishers and authors? Are they becoming a regular part of book marketing?

Steve: Absolutely, they're becoming very popular among authors who handle their own publicity, and professional book consultants are jumping on the bandwagon too. Blogs are the place where people who are passionate about something gather to exchange ideas. So there's no better place for an author to start a discussion and get people excited about his or her book.

FPP: What is the best way to find good blogs on which to appear?

Steve: Perhaps you already read a blog that covers your genre or topic area. But it never hurts to look for new blogs, because they can spring up seemingly overnight and gain popularity quickly. Unfortunately, there's no authoritative directory or listing of blogs divided into neat categories. You just have to research it for yourself. Three sites are good starting places for your search:

Technorati. This blog tracking site lists the 100 most popular blogs at Technorati.com/pop/blogs. But to find niche content, you'll need to look beyond the mainstream. Use the advanced search tool.

To drill down into specific topics try these sites:

Google Blog Search. Type in keywords related to your book. Ignore results from personal blogs that focus on the author and get little traffic.

Forbes' Best of the Web. This directory reviews blogs with high-quality content. Also, some of the popular, general book blogs have "blogrolls" on their sidebars, which are long lists of other quality book blogs. For example, scroll down the right side of the blog *Grumpy Old Bookman.*

That blogroll has links to dozens and dozens of great book blogs, and in turn, those blogs link to more far-flung niche blogs. Also, the blogs you pitch don't necessarily need to be a "book blog." Especially if your book is nonfiction, you'll find lots of opportunities at all kinds blogs that target people who care about your topic.

FPP: How should an author or publisher approach a blog owner about an interview?

Steve: Send a personal e-mail to the publisher or blog author. Offer to send a review copy of the book, and explain why this will provide interesting content for the blog's readers. This is a win-win for the blog author because they get free content that provides value for their readership.

FPP: How many blogs should a tour include?

Steve: It all depends on how big your niche is. You should ask to appear on every blog in your topic area or genre that gets appreciable traffic. Look at how many reader comments the blog attracts, that's a sign of an engaged audience.

FPP: How much time should an author or publisher expect to invest in setting up a tour?

Steve: It can easily take a week or two. It's also a good idea to prepare a book excerpt or HTML document that can serve as sort of an online book flyer. The excerpt can be posted a few days before your appearances at the various blogs to publicize your appearance and get the dicussion going. I explain this in some detail in my book "Plug Your Book," where you can see an example of an excerpt.

FPP: What things should an author do to prepare for an interview?

Steve: It's helpful to read the previous few weeks of postings to the blogs you're going to appear on. Since you're the author, you're the expert on your book. Just remember to be diplomatic, and if you get rude or off-topic comments, steer the discussion back to the points you want to discuss.

FPP: How can the effectiveness of a blog tour be measured, if at all?

Steve: The only way to measure the results is by posting an affiliate or tracking link, which enables you to see the book sales resulting from a specific site. The blog owner might allow you to post your own affiliate link, but they might want to post their own links to *Amazon*, for example, so that they earn a commission (and that's fair). It's always been terribly hard to track book sales, because they depend on word of mouth.

FPP: Do you see any new trends emerging in the use of virtual book tours?

Steve: I think a lot of people are catching on to this method of marketing, in the book industry and in other areas. Consumers just don't pay much attention to traditional advertising anymore. You've got to show up at the places where they are already discussing something that matters to them, like blogs. It's getting a lot easier to put audio and video content on blogs, so this will undoubtedly be a trend to watch. Virtual book tours in the future will go beyond plain text, and into spoken-word interviews, book readings, and visual performances.

Summary

Blog touring is an exciting new way for authors to utilize the Internet to discover potential new readers. It offers a cost effective alternative to traditional book tours and at the same time provides greater exposure for the author's work.

In this chapter, we examined the tools and techniques you need to set up, manage and analyze your own blog tour. In chapter 9, we will explore another web-based book marketing tool, the book video or book "trailer." This tool provides a powerful, but more generalized way to reach a broad spectrum of prospective customers for your title.

9
Make a Book Trailer

In his insightful work on the development of the book cover during the twentieth century, *Front Cover: Great Book Jacket and Cover Design*, Alan Powers chronicles the evolution of the book cover from simple protective dust jacket to critical marketing component and charts the cultural influences that shaped its design. Today the book cover remains one of the most important marketing devices to lure potential buyers.

But now a new marketing tool is taking its place alongside the venerable book cover. It is the book *trailer* also known as a *book wrap* or a *book video*. A book trailer is usually a 2-3 minute video featuring author interviews and visuals which illustrate the content of the book. Book trailers are showing up on *YouTube* and other online video distribution sites where they serve a dual purpose as entertainment and advertising. In just a few years, the book trailer has emerged as a "must have" in the book marketing mix.

Emergence of the Book Trailer

The power of this new marketing tool was demonstrated when Harper Perennial, a paperback unit of HarperCollins publishing, produced 3 videos which were posted on *YouTube* as part of its promotion campaign for *The Average American Male*. During a two week period in March, 2007, the videos received over 1 million views according to the Wall Street Journal. That is major exposure by anyone's standard!

Forces that are driving its popularity include the following:

- Publishers are looking for new ways to promote their titles in a crowded market

- Publishers need new ways to engage a new, media savvy generation of readers
- 72% of users are now connecting to the Internet with broadband
- Book trailers offer a less expensive way to market books

Compared to some forms of book marketing, book trailers are not cheap. Costs can range from $2,000 to $5,000+ depending on the production values the author or publisher decides to add. But they can serve many functions. Book trailers can be used as a means to secure print and TV media coverage; in conjunction with virtual book tours; web ads (in a shortened format); as sales videos for major retailers; as presales material to book buyers; for in store video loops; and as book club promotions.

Several video production houses now specialize in creating book trailers. For example, *Bookstream, Inc., Circle of Seven Productions and Expanded Books*. And, there are now book trailer awards, e.g., the Book Standard's Book Video Awards.

Producers of book trailers have to balance creating strong cinematic appeal with still allowing readers the freedom to conjure up their own mental imagery. For as we all know, sometimes the movie doesn't measure up to the book. Like the book cover before it, the book trailer will evolve into an art form influenced by commercial needs, reader expectations, and the ambient culture, but with its own rules and artistic devices.

Planning a Book Trailer

Once you have made the decision to create a book trailer, there are several items you will want to consider.

- Audience
- Message
- Treatment
- Available assets
- Budget
- Schedule

Individuals find book videos much the same way they find anything on the Internet, that is, by typing key words and phrases into search engines. Part of your audience planning involves creating tags for your book trailer that will match up to these key words and phrases. You may want to design these so that the audience for your book trailer is broader than the readership of your blog. This will help you discover new audience segments.

Creative Brief

The *creative brief* is especially helpful in developing a book video, whether you are doing it yourself or contracting it to someone else. A creative brief is a short document that helps you define the purpose, audience, and message of your book video.

A creative brief can be formulated by answering the following series of questions:

1. What is the primary purpose of the book video?
2. What is unique about this author and / or the book?
3. Who are the primary and secondary audiences for the book video?
4. What is the primary motivation of each audience?
5. Describe the main idea the book video must communicate.
6. Describe the impact you want to have on the viewer or the action you want the viewer to take as a result of watching your book trailer.
7. Describe any mandatory elements or graphics that should be used in the book video.

Providing answers to these questions will go a long way toward helping you produce a successful book video, whether doing it yourself or contracting it to another firm or individual.

Treatment

The book *video treatment* describes the creative elements that will be employed to achieve the results outlined in the creative brief. The treatment will outline:

- High level storyboard
- Mood
- Location
- Characters

- Graphics or animation
- Music
- Lighting
- Narration / voiceover

The treatment helps the budgeting and scheduling process. Some elements of the book video may need to be created, acquired and / or licensed. If your budget cannot accommodate all of the elements identified in your treatment, you will need to make tradeoffs between cost and production values.

Script

The script provides the narrative for the action taking place in the book video. The script includes any narration as well as dialogue spoken by the characters that appear. In the case of an author interview, a script may not be necessary except to define the questions being asked.

A simple script can be created by using a two column table format. The left column contains the narrative voiceover, characters' dialogue, or music; the right column describes the action taking place on the screen. Each row defines a specific view or scene.

You may also add a third column which contains timing, but this is usually not necessary during the planning stages. Timing can be added later when you have the talent read the script.

Book Trailer Distribution

Once you have created your book trailer, you will need to make it available online. Today, the distribution is greatly aided by the plethora of online video sites like *YouTube*. You can manage the process of uploading and tracking you video yourself, or use services set up for that purpose.

One such service is *Tube Mogul* (www.tubemogul.com). Tube Mogul will distribute your video to as many as 35 sites and give you tools to help track your book trailer campaign (see "Tracking" below).

Another approach to distributing your video is the use of a book video production company that also provides marketing and distribution services. One example is *Circle of Seven Productions* (www.cosproductions.com). The advantage of using a book video production company is that they can often provide better audience targeting for your book video.

Distribution sites run the gamut from broad-based to highly specialized. *YouTube* is great for getting wide exposure, but there may be specialty video distribution sites that appeal directly to the audience your book is striving to reach. These sites may be specialized in terms of audience, genre, or channel.

One genre-specialized site is *Romance Novel TV* (www.romancenovel.tv). As its name implies, the site only features book videos based on romance novels. If you had written a romance novel and wanted to show your book video to a receptive audience with a high likelihood of purchasing your book, Romance Novel TV would be a great choice.

The websites of large bookstore chains like Borders and Barnes and Noble, and some large independent bookstores like Powell's Books in Portland, OR, now feature book videos of top selling titles. This is an example of channel-based distribution. The emergence of the Internet-capable, video-enabled mobile phone opens up another exciting possibility for distributing your book video. This is especially important because the number of mobile phones vastly exceeds the number of personal computers worldwide and offers a larger audience and one that may better reflect the audience you are trying to reach.

Tracking Your Book Trailer

Once you have launched your book video campaign, monitor how many people are viewing it, as well as other important information. There are a number of useful book video metrics available, and most of the marketing and distribution services we discussed earlier provide these for you. Here are some basic measurements to use in determining whether your campaign is a success:

- Total views (across multiple sites)
- Number of comments
- Ratings

These basic measurements may be trended over time to give you a general idea of how successful the campaign is at attracting viewers. Some distribution services also offer more sophisticated monitoring, including:

- Blogs and websites linking to your videos
- Audience demographics: gender, age, household income, ethnicity, education and household size
- Geographic location of the viewers watching your videos
- "Buzz" tracking. This means tracking videos and viewership across the internet based upon selected keywords; buzz includes what is being said about your video as well as other videos using similar keywords.

The more in depth package of metrics may cost you a premium over the price for basic services. It is useful to correlate events occurring in your other book marketing activities with changes in your book video analytics. For example, if you are giving a talk about your book or holding a book signing at a bookstore, try to see if these events have an impact on your book video viewership.

Should You Try to Produce your Own?

The question often comes up about whether an author should produce his or her own book trailer. After all, excellent tools for producing video are available for free or at low cost. You can easily upload your book video to any number of free video websites. So, why not do it yourself and save the money?

All of these arguments make good sense if you can answer the following questions affirmatively:

- Do you know how to design a book video that effectively delivers your book's message to viewers with very short attention spans?
- Can you produce a high quality video with the tools you have?
- Can you (or do you want to) invest the time to find and distribute your book trailer to sites that cater to your readers, monitor the results, and adapt your strategy as necessary.

To make the determination objectively, put a dollar value on your time and be realistic in assessing the time it will take if you answered "no" or "maybe" to any one of these questions. You may find that it makes better economic sense to find a firm with a proven track record to do the job for you.

Summary

The book trailer or book video, has evolved from an interesting curiosity to an important element in the book marketing mix, much as the book cover did at the beginning of the Twentieth century.

In this chapter, we have covered the basics of planning, producing, distributing, and tracking a book trailer. There are many factors to take into consideration when deciding whether to make your own book trailer or have someone else do it for you. Certainly, the tools necessary to produce a video have become much more affordable, making it possible for individuals to create their own book trailers. However, the most important considerations are how much of your own time do you want to invest, and do you have the creative chops to produce a book video that others will find engaging.

The book trailer does not stand by itself. It is one component of an overall book marketing campaign. The use of book videos should be coordinated with your other book marketing activities. Ultimately, your goal is to create a community around your work and, in the process, garner more book sales. In the next chapter, we will look at some authors who have done this to perfection and explore how you can use their example to build your own community of readers.

10
Build a Community

Some authors have gone well beyond establishing an online readership for their work. These men and women have achieved an almost cult status with large and devoted followings. They have built *communities* of readers where there is not only interaction between author and readers, but among readers themselves. Being a member of the community becomes important in and of itself.

In this chapter, we will examine three examples of authors that have built robust publishing franchises based on the support of their vibrant, online fan bases.

Max Quick: A Four Quadrant Hit

Most of us have enough on our hands just keeping up with our day jobs. But Mark Jeffrey, author of the ultra popular Max Quick series of books and podcast audiobooks has two day jobs. His first podiobook, *Max Quick 1: The Pocket and the Pendant*, has received over 2 million downloads to date. And he is currently CTO of *Mahalo.com*, a human-powered search service. Previously, Mark co-founded *ZeroDegrees*, a business social network (sold to IAC/InterActiveCorp in 2004). He was CEO and co-founder of *SuperSig* in 1999. Mark also co-founded *The Palace, Inc.*, an early (1995) avatar chat platform backed by *Intel, Time Warner* and *Softbank* with 10 million users (sold to Communities.com in 1998). Mark lives in Santa Monica, California.

In an interview with *Future Perfect Publishing*, Mark talked about the elements that went into the building of the Max Quick reader community. First, he focused on an area of publishing he felt was being underserved, the young adult, or "YA" market.

"Initially, [I wrote the Max Quick series] because it was something I thought I could do, that it was within my abilities as a first-time writer. I thought I would start with a 'toy world' and graduate from there to more serious stuff. But I quickly realized that I had actually, unwittingly, begun writing in one of the most serious of worlds possible. Paradoxically, it's adult fiction that is usually rather trivial. Think about it. Who's zooming who, who killed who -- it's all the same stuff, over and over. But Young Adult (YA) deals with large, archetypal themes. We are dealing with stories from the collective unconscious. That's explosive. That's handling nitro, baby.

"There is a certain marketing logic to YA. The movie industry whispers in awe about a 'four quadrant' hit, one that appeals to young and old, men and women equally. Good YA is likewise 'four quadrant.' It has much more hit potential than anything narrowly focused. Why? Because it is archetypal. It is universal and timeless, at least when it is done correctly."[29]

Mr. Jeffrey also applied his experience as a social networking entrepreneur to the task of marketing the Max Quick series in ways that resonated with his young audience.

"The Max Quick Series has been marketed in many innovative ways, and was among the first in each case. And that can be directly traced to my 'DNA as an Internet Guy', if you will. I released the book first via Lulu.com in 2004 as a self-published paper book and as a downloadable PDF. In the beginning of 2005, *Max Quick 1: The Pocket and the Pendant* was one of the very first podiobooks ever released. I also released 'Pocket' on the Kindle. And most recently, 'Pocket' and *Max Quick 2: The Two Travelers* were both released in the iPhone App Store."[30]

Over time, he found new methods to engage with his readers and fans.

"A lot people follow me on Twitter and friend up with me on Facebook these days. Some people email me. It never gets old, either. I love hearing what people think about the series, the good and the bad. I love hearing how they found out about it. It's still sort of something that you have to discover somehow on your own.

"In the second edition of 'Pocket' I included a lot of fan art that people sent in to me. Most of it is quite good! There are some seriously good artists reading the books!"[31]

He encourages writers, especially beginning writers, to not limit themselves by traditional conceptions of the book and book publishing.

"Take advantage of the new distribution mediums! Own your own future! Get it out on Lulu.com, the Kindle (why not?), iPhone, PDF, podiobooks.com, whatever. Your problem is not that you're not rich. Your problem is nobody has ever heard of you before. It's a privilege that someone else will take the time to read your stuff.

"Also, the definition of what a book actually *is* ... is pretty fluid now. It's more like software. For example, what is out right now for 'Pocket'? I consider 'Pocket 1.0'. I may do a 'Pocket 2.0' with expanded scenes, new scenes, etc. I may double the length of it, like an extended edition DVD. There's a lot of things I wanted to do with the journey across America that I could not get to and remain under 100,000 words. Now that there are so many fans of the book, I feel I have permission to expand it. There's no reason not to.

"I may release the first six chapters for free in the iPhone App Store (in fact I probably will) like a sampler game level.

"The point is: we are no longer in a world where you publish it and it is set in stone for eternity. You can keep upgrading it. You have to be careful so you don't destroy the illusion of continuity. You can't be completely fluid to the point of silliness (for example, in the newer 'Star Wars', Lucas has Greedo fire at Han Solo first -- and miss at point blank range! -- that is silliness, don't change your stuff THAT much).

"Finally, your early audience can help you write your book. Readers have found consistency errors in the earlier version of Pocket that I've since corrected. They are basically beta testers. Take their feedback, fix your book, re-release it. Scott Sigler, JC Hutchins (*7th Son*) Matthew Wayne Selznick (*Brave Men Run*) have commented on this at length. The audience can help you write. Take advantage of that. Again, books are more like software now."[32]

When asked whether the free podcast downloads of his books had added to or detracted from sales of the print version, he was quick to respond:

"Definitely added. The free podcasts have gotten over 2.3 million downloads. And as a direct result, Oscar-nominee Abigail Breslin (Little Miss Sunshine) heard the podcasts and recently called it one of her favorite books. Which was great marketing, of course…nothing better than one of the top child actors in the world saying nice things about your books!"[33]

Public Secrets: Frank Warren

Some of the most successful blogs go beyond becoming a published title with content from blog posts. They turn into a full fledged community that actively participates in helping the blog author create content. One of the best examples of this is *PostSecret.*, which we introduced briefly in Chapter 5. *PostSecret* was started by Frank Warren a few years ago as an art project. The project has spawned a blog, four wildly popular books (*PostSecret, My Secret, The Secret Lives of Men and Women* and *PostSecret: Extraordinary Confessions from Ordinary Lives*), an art show and a very active community with a helpline. Content from his site, in the form of postcards, has been featured on MTV in a music video. He has been featured on *USA Today*, CNN and made numerous appearances on television talk shows. He is slated to produce four more books and created a video about *PostSecret.*

Here's how it works. Visitors can share a secret by creating a postcard and mailing it (yes, "snail mail") to an address in Germantown, Maryland. The blog is updated with new secrets every Sunday. According to *Ovation*, Mr. Warren receives about 100 - 200 postcards per day and has collected over 100,000 postcards since starting the blog.[34] Many of the postcards are very artfully done. His site receives over 3,000,000 visitors every month. The site also features a "Hopeline" where individuals can receive phone counseling. The secrets featured on PostSecret cover a full spectrum of human activities, interests and foibles. There is probably something for everyone within the collection of secrets.

What is interesting about *PostSecret's* success is that it illustrates some of the elements of a blog that foster community:

- An enhanced ability to interact in a unique way, in this case via physical postcards
- Opportunity for audience members to see their "content" reflected on the blog as well as others' reactions to it
- Creation of permanent "keepsakes," for example, the printed books that have resulted from the blog
- Sense of shared experiences among the participants
- Ability to engage a larger, non-participating crowd of "lurkers"

PostSecret is a prime example of how blogs can evolve from a publishing medium to a center for a loyal and active community.

Social Vampires: Stephenie Meyer

The July 31, 2008, issue of *BusinessWeek* put the spotlight on social media as an effective force in helping to drive book sales. In the article, "The Online Fan World of the Twilight Vampire Books,"[35] Heather Green chronicled the manner in which Stephenie Meyer, a 34-year-old mother of three from Phoenix, built a huge fan base for her work using a variety of social media sites and tools. Meyer has written four books (the *Twilight Saga*) featuring two star-crossed lovers, Edward Cullen (a handsome vampire) and Bella Swan (a teenage girl living in Forks, Washington). The final book in the series, *Breaking Dawn*, was released August 2, 2008. The book has an initial print run of 3.2 million copies. Overall, sales of books in the series have topped 7.5 million copies. The film adaptation, *Twilight*, was released in theaters December 12, 2008. In the meantime, numerous Twilight videos (including the official movie trailer) have appeared on YouTube and other video sites.

Her story and characters were inspired by a dream. She describes it on her website:

"In my dream, two people were having an intense conversation in a meadow in the woods. One of these people was just your average girl. The other person was fantastically beautiful, sparkly, and a vampire. They were discussing the difficulties inherent in the facts that A) they were falling in love with each other while, B) the vampire was particularly attracted to the scent of her blood, and was having a difficult time restraining himself from killing her immediately."

Her location for the saga was somewhat less inspired, the result of some research on Google.

"For my setting, I knew I needed someplace ridiculously rainy. I turned to Google, as I do for all my research needs, and looked for the place with the most rainfall in the U.S. This turned out to be the Olympic Peninsula in Washington State. I pulled up maps of the area and studied them, looking for something small, out of the way, surrounded by forest... And there, right where

I wanted it to be, was a tiny town called "Forks." It couldn't have been more perfect if I had named it myself."

But it was her efforts to build an audience for her books that was truly inspired. Here are some of the extra steps that Meyer took to develop this community.

- **Personal website.** She created a website for her novels separate from the publisher's book site

- **Fan access.** Meyer gave readers her personal e-mail and shared family photos on her website.

- **Active community sites.** Enthusiastic readers have built up a large number of fan sites that help drive sales of Meyer's books. On her website, Meyer lists over 100 fan sites, including 5 in languages other than English.

- **Fan content.** Allowing, even encouraging fans to play with the content.

- **Events.** For the launch of *Breaking Dawn*, Meyer helped organize a kind of vampire prom night in multiple cities. This kind of event reinforces the community experience for fans.

In terms of community-building, Stephenie Meyer does many of the same things as J.C. Hutchins (*Seventh Son*) and Frank Warren (*Post Secret*). What lessons can writers draw from her success? There is no magic formula for the mega success of the *Twilight Saga*. Many genres may have the networks of inspired enthusiasts necessary to match Twilight's level of success. But here are some things that could probably benefit any aspiring writer.

- Engage potential fans early and often; access is important though it may not be sustainable if you become hyper-successful

- Go to the sites and forums where your readers hang out

- Let your fans play a role in defining your brand

None of these steps is easy; all are time consuming. But an author's most important job is building an audience. The good news is that these days there are plenty of good social networking tools to make that job easier.

Interview with Grammar Girl Mignon Fogarty

Mignon Fogarty produces one of the most popular podcasts (or audio blog) in the United States, called *Grammar Girl*. Her podcasts get hundreds of thousands of downloads each week. As its title hints, Grammar Girl is a weekly lesson in some particular aspect of good grammar. She has recently authored a CD and a book by the same title. She has also created a franchise of fourteen other advice podcasts (e.g., *Money Girl*, *Mighty Mommy*, *Legal Lad*, *Nutrition Diva*, etc.) under the umbrella brand *Quick & Dirty Tips*.

In August 2007, Future Perfect Publishing interviewed Ms. Fogarty about her experiences and lessons learned from the creation of Grammar Girl.[36] It is republished here as a good example of how a blog in one medium (audio) can translate into another (book).

FPP: Were you always interested in grammar?

Mignon: I bought all the popular grammar books as they came out over the years, but I can't say I was always a grammar fanatic. I do love working on it now though; it's fascinating.

FPP: What inspired you to start the Grammar Girl podcast?

Mignon: I was working as a science and technical writer back in 2005 and ended up starting a weekly podcast about science. That show did well - it won the Best Science Show category of the Podcast Peer Awards - but it became a huge drain on my time. Each show took at least 10 hours to produce, and although the traffic probably put the show in the top 20% of all podcasts, it clearly wasn't ever going to become my main source of income.

So I began to think about other ways I could stay in podcasting without it being such a time sink. I came up with six or seven ideas for short tip-based shows, and as I was editing technical documents one day at the coffee shop, looking at grammar error after grammar error, I was finally inspired to choose grammar as the theme. I scribbled down about four possible episode topics, threw up a website, and recorded the first Grammar Girl podcast..

FPP: Grammar Girl is one of the most popular podcasts now. Grammar seems like an unlikely topic to have such wide appeal. To what do you attribute its popularity?

Mignon: I know what you mean; I was surprised by the popularity too.

The messages I receive from listeners and the interactions I have with people in general have led me to a few conclusions. First, there is a bigger population of language lovers than you might imagine.

Second, everyone seems to have a language question they've always wondered about but never bothered to investigate. I get a lot of e-mail messages that start out "I've always wondered . . ."

Third, because of e-mail and instant messaging, I believe people are writing more now than in previous years. Whereas 20 years ago people would pick up a phone and call a business contact, today it's more common to write an e-mail message. Schools don't spend a lot of time on language rules, so people feel insecure about their writing. When they see that there is an easy, fun way to learn the practical little rules, they get excited.

FPP: What's the makeup of your audience and why are they so interested in grammar?

Mignon: Based on surveys I've done, my audience is about half male and half female. Listeners tend to be highly educated, have good incomes, and range in age from 25 to 45.

In general, the people I hear from say the show helps them do better at work or at school.

FPP: Before you began podcasting, you were a writer. What things did you have to learn when you made the transition to audio and first began podcasting?

Mignon: I didn't know anything about audio production or writing for audio when I first started, so I had a lot of learning to do. I had to learn what kind of equipment and software to use and then how to use it. I picked up everything I know from reading websites and forums and from experimenting. That's probably why it took me so long to produce the science podcast!

FPP: What made you choose audio vs. print as your format to teach people about grammar?

Mignon: I was already committed to doing an audio show, so it was really more a matter of choosing grammar as a topic than choosing a format for teaching grammar.

FPP: You've created a new audiobook "Grammar Girl's Quick and Dirty Tips." Are you considering a print version as well?

Mignon: I'm working on a print book that should come out in time for the back-to-school season next year.

FPP: What is involved in putting an episode together and what is your time commitment on a weekly basis to the show?

Mignon: First I choose a topic. The topics almost always come from listener questions, and when it's possible I like to tie the show to a current event. For example, when Hillary Clinton picked "You and I" for her campaign song, I used that as a jumping off point to talk about the phrase "between you and I," which a lot of listeners had asked about.

Once I have the topic I do a lot of research. I have about 20 reference books and I also do Internet searches. Even if I think I know the answer, I check as many references as I can to make sure I'm not missing something. Depending on how complicated the topic is, research can go quickly or it can take many hours. More than once I've abandoned a topic after hours of research because it ends up feeling too complicated to cover in a five-minute podcast.

Once I'm comfortable with what I want to say, I write my script and then send it to a copy editor for review. Sometimes when I get the script back there is some back-and-forth with the copy editor about minor points of grammar. And when the script is done I record the show.

I'd like to get ahead, but I'm not; so right now I tend to work right up to the Thursday night deadline. So depending on how late it is, I either send my audio file to my sound guy for editing or (if it is too late) I edit it and post it myself.

I'd say the whole process takes 8 hours for a very easy show and 20 hours for a very complicated show or when I have to abandon a topic and start over.

FPP: What has worked well and what things have you had to change during the life of Grammar Girl?

Mignon: When I was just starting out I didn't always put references on the website. I put up references now because I found that doing so heads off criticism from people who think they know the rules but are misinformed. I found that if I didn't post my references, I would often end up going back and citing them anyway to defend my position.

FPP: How do you measure the success of your podcast?

Mignon: I track audio file downloads, web page views, rankings, and listener questions, and all of those metrics would support the idea that the podcast is successful, but for me personally it's the listener feedback that makes me feel as if the show is successful. For example, Grammar Girl is one of the most reviewed podcasts at iTunes; people seem to like the show so much that they spontaneously take the time to write reviews, and I'm very moved by that.

FPP: How does Grammar Girl earn money? Has it become easier to attract advertisers?

Mignon: I make money primarily by having advertising in the podcast, and it has definitely been easier over time to attract advertisers. Not only has Grammar Girl become more well known over the last year, but advertisers are also becoming more comfortable with podcasting.

I also released an audiobook in March that's done very well. It was originally available as a download from *iTunes* and *Audible*, and it came out on CD in July. The title is Grammar Girl's Quick and Dirty Tips to Clean Up Your Writing.

FPP: Has the rapid growth in your listening population changed the way you do your podcast and handle your interactions with the audience?

Mignon: The rapid growth was overwhelming at first because I was still working as a technical writer. At first I tried to personally answer every listener question, but I get a lot of long, complicated grammar questions and answering them all quickly became impossible.

I started keeping a handwritten list of questions, which became a Word document with questions, which finally became a spreadsheet that I use to organize questions in a way that makes it easy to find topics I want to use for the show.

I was able to quit working as a technical writer in January to focus on podcasting full time, and it became more manageable after that. I still can't answer every question personally, but I do try to answer as many as I can.

FPP: What's in store for the future of Grammar Girl?

Mignon: My top priority is still putting out a new Grammar Girl episode every week. I'm just plugging through listener questions.

"You might recall that I said I just threw up the original Grammar Girl website, so it's not a surprise that it isn't very pretty or user-friendly. So I'm working on redesigning the website to make it easier to use and search. That should be done in September. As I said, there is the print book that will come out next year, and of course, I'm always working on growing the Quick and Dirty Tips podcast network."

Good Practices for Community Building

What can you learn from these examples about building your own community of rabid fans?

First, understand your audience. Once you have identified your writing niche, explore the sites, forums and networks where your prospective fans hang out. The Internet provides a very robust set of search tools to help you identify these groups. For example, if you are writing fiction and want to understand your future readers better, find similar existing books on *Amazon.com*, then do Google searches on those titles to find the book sites, fan sites and blogs talking about those titles. This can tell you a lot about how to engage with your future audience.

Second, once you have readers, allow them to have access to you and your work. This can be difficult for many authors who are used to working in a solitary mode. Balance your solitary writing time with time for interacting with your readers. Their enthusiasm should more than provide the energy you need.

Third, encourage your readers to help you participate in the work. Encourage them to create derivative content and share it with other fans. For example, J.C. Hutchins' fans have created *7th Son* merchandise that they sell on his website and blog. Stephenie Meyer has encouraged her fans to create "mash ups" from the chapters of her book and post them to fan sites. Frank Warren lets his fans see the content they created and others' reactions to it on his *PostSecret* site and in his books. All of these deepen reader involvement and give them incentives to spread the word about your writing.

Finally, don't be afraid to expand your work using new technologies. Today, your writing can be in a printed book, an e-book, serialized in e-mails or podcasts, displayed on mobile phones—and this list is certain to grow as our society finds new ways to communicate and share information.

Summary

In this chapter, we have looked at the strategies available to you to build a robust community for your work. The social networking tools that have become so popular in the last several years provide a variety of ways to build such communities. You should take the time to learn about and adapt these tools in helping to build your readership. In the future, they will certainly be a necessary component of every author's marketing toolkit.

Appendix A
Blog Planning Tools

Creating a successful blog requires careful planning. This appendix provides several planning tools and checklists you can use to plan your blog.

The tools provided here will help you:

- Define your blog's identity
- Research blogs on similar or related topics
- Track and trend your blog's key metrics

Define Your Blog's Identity

Name of your blog
Have you checked for blogs with similar or duplicate names? ☐ Yes   ☐ No
Topic of your blog
Write a short (2-3 sentence) description of your blog
List 10 keywords that relate to this topic 1. 2. 3. 4. 5. 6. 7. 8. 9. 10.
List 10 subtopics or article titles for your blog 1. 2. 3. 4. 5. 6. 7. 8. 9. 10.

Research Related Blogs

(fill out one form for each blog researched)

Blog name	
Blog author(s)	
Topic / description	
Technorati blog authority	
Categories (if applicable)	

Commercial?	☐ Yes	☐ No	If yes:
Contextual ads	☐ Yes	☐ No	
Sponsored ads	☐ Yes	☐ No	
Affiliate programs	☐ Yes	☐ No	
Products	☐ Yes	☐ No	
Services	☐ Yes	☐ No	

Describe nature / number of comments

Blog Content Metrics Worksheet

(fill out one form for each month)

Month / year:
Total words: (# words in posts + # words in comments +# words in pages)
Book equivalents: (# total words / 90,000)
Average post length: (# total words in posts / # posts)
Average comments per post: (# comments / # posts)
Content distribution by category: Category _____________________ # Posts _____ # Comments _____   Category _____________________ # Posts _____ # Comments _____   Category _____________________ # Posts _____ # Comments _____   Category _____________________ # Posts _____ # Comments _____   Category _____________________ # Posts _____ # Comments _____   Category _____________________ # Posts _____ # Comments _____   Category _____________________ # Posts _____ # Comments _____   Category _____________________ # Posts _____ # Comments _____   Category _____________________ # Posts _____ # Comments _____   Category _____________________ # Posts _____ # Comments _____   Category _____________________ # Posts _____ # Comments _____   Category _____________________ # Posts _____ # Comments _____   Category _____________________ # Posts _____ # Comments _____   Category _____________________ # Posts _____ # Comments _____   Category _____________________ # Posts _____ # Comments _____   Category _____________________ # Posts _____ # Comments _____   Category _____________________ # Posts _____ # Comments _____
Author load: (total posts / # authors)

Blog Traffic Metrics Worksheet

(fill out one form for each month)

Month / year:
Total visitors: __________ Unique visitors: __________
Total feed subscribers: __________ Unique feed subscribers: __________ Average daily feed subscribers: __________ (total feed subscribers / 30 days)
Overall blog traffic: __________ (total visitors + total feed subscribers) Unique blog readership: __________ (total unique visitors + total unique feed subscribers)
List of significant events that may have increased / decreased traffic: Date ______   Event ____ Date ______   Event ____ Date ______   Event ____ Date ______   Event ____ Date ______   Event ____ Date ______   Event ____ Date ______   Event ____ Date ______   Event ____ Date ______   Event ____ Date ______   Event ____ Date ______   Event ____ Date ______   Event ____ Date ______   Event ____ Date ______   Event ____ Date ______   Event ____ Date ______   Event ____ Date ______   Event ____

Appendix B
Useful Blogging Practices

In the table below, you will find a list of useful blogging practices with descriptions, grouped into the following categories :

- Blog design
- Content design
- Posting practices
- Linking practices
- Community participation
- Blog management

BLOG DESIGN	
Meaningful name	Select a name and tagline for your blog that clearly reflects the topic and incorporates at least one of your keywords.
Attractive, functional design	Whether you are using a blog content management system, e.g., *WordPress.com*, *Blogger.com*, or *TypePad*, or a custom solution, it is important to have a design that makes it easy for visitors to find the information they are seeking. This includes factors like fonts that are easy to read onscreen. Other factors are interesting and relevant graphics, and access to posts in multiple ways, such as calendar-based, category-based, and a top-10 post list. If you are unsure about the types of design touches that can add value to your blog, it is worth the investment to consult a professional designer.
Good use of keywords	New visitors to your site are most likely to locate you by entering a keyword or phrase into a search engine. It is a good idea to have a set of keywords that characterize your blog's topic space to use consistently in your blog title, post titles, category names, and post content. There are a number of tools to choose from to research keywords:

	Keyword Discovery, *WordTracker*, *SitePoint*, and *SEOBook* are just a few. Each of these tools provides an estimate of the number of searches being made with your chosen keyword and suggests related keywords to use. The best keywords are those closely related to your topic, but not so popular as to generate an overwhelming number of search results. Create a blog name and rich categories that reference the keywords in your glossary. Sprinkle those keywords liberally throughout your posts.
Judicious use of advertising	It is probably a good idea to wait until your blog has achieved a certain level of readership before you start advertising. Ads, whether they are sponsorships, banners, contextual, or other, can produce annoying clutter and may have a negative impact on the number of readers who subscribe to your blog, add you to their favorites list, or link to you from their sites. Take the time to carefully integrate advertising into the design of your blog so the ads will not offend or overly distract your audience.
Use categories	Most blog software does not require you to use categories. However, categories can help you organize your content into subject or topic areas that are meaningful for readers. Categories also help to "amplify" the amount of content you appear to have on your blog, since a single post can be included in multiple categories.
CONTENT DESIGN	
Focus	Decide who you are writing for and what you are going to write about, then stick to it. Do not load up the blog with posts on unrelated topics. A blog with multiple topics is disorienting, not just to readers that stumble upon it, but to the search engines as well. Not only does a very specific topic make your blog search engine friendly and result in higher rankings, but it also provides the chance to build your profile as an expert in your field. In no time, readers will be coming to your blog for their regular dose of your wisdom. The more highly focused your blogging niche, the better.
Tagging	A tag is a category name that helps to classify the content of your post. Many of the hosted and custom blog platforms provide the ability to create categories and assign posts to them. If yours does not, you can add these via HTML. They appear as special links in blog posts with the tag embedded. *Technorati* is the first place that you should be tagging posts. Put the tags right on your page, pointing to

	the *Technorati* searches that you are targeting. There are other good places to ping, *del.icio.us* and *Flickr* being the two most obvious. Tagging content can also be valuable to help give a traffic boost from big referral sites such as *Reddit, Digg* and *StumbleUpon*. Do not submit every post to these sites, but some reasonable percentage is worth your while (say 5 percent).
Authenticity	People like empathy, compassion, authority, and honesty. Keep these in the forefront of your mind when writing and you will be in a good position to succeed. It is also critical to sustain a level of humility in your blogging and stick to your roots. When users start to feel that a blog is taking itself too seriously or losing the characteristics that made it unique, they start to seek new places for content. Be cautious to control not only what you say, but how you say it. If there is a hot button issue that has you posting emotionally, temper it by letting the post sit in draft mode for an hour or two. Re-read it, and consider any revisions you want to make.
Easy bookmarking	Adding content features like widgets or buttons with labels like "add to del.icio.us" are one way to make the process of tagging pages easier. Be certain pages include a list of relevant tags and suggested notes for a link (which come up automatically when you go to tag a site). Make sure to tag pages first on popular social bookmarking sites, including more than just your homepage.
Topics worth covering	In every area, there are topics that may not get as much coverage as they deserve. Finding these content gaps requires time and effort to research, synthesize, and present in a coherent and compelling way. But this is exactly the reason that individuals spend time reading blogs – to get information that is hard to find elsewhere. Your investment in producing this type of link-worthy content will help attract new visitors and subscribers.
Content that travels	Examine your content and look for opportunities to package it into handy downloads. This can include such things as resource lists, FAQs, whitepapers, and products reviews. Be sure to always include links back to your blog in any content that will be downloaded or otherwise shared. When you have content that is portable (such as PDFs, video files and audio files), submitting them to relevant sites will help your content travel further, and ultimately drive

	links back to your blog.
POSTING PRACTICES	
Develop a pre-publish checklist	Here are a few things you should definitely do before publishing your post: • Read the entire post aloud; this will immediately alert you to any awkward sentence fragments. • Run a spell check. Most blogging platforms provide this function. If not, do it manually, or, if you are not confident about your own spelling skills, ask someone for assistance with the proofreading. • Check all your links to be sure they really work. It can be irritating for readers to click on a link that gives a "site not found error." • Preview your post before publishing to ensure that images, text, and links display as you intended.
Go beyond text	Blogs that contain nothing but line after line of text are more difficult to read and less consistently interesting than those offering images, interactive elements, the occasional multimedia content, and some charts and graphs. Even if you are having a tough time with non-text content, think about how you can format the text using block quotes, indentation, bullet points, etc., to create a more visually appealing and digestible block of content.
Post at a consistent frequency	Key to building an audience is setting reader expectations about when you will post next. Don't attempt to post too frequently at first. Focus on posting on a consistent basis, whether it is three times a week, once a week, or once a month.
Refer back to previous posts	After you have built up a body of posts, it is a good idea to set up "Related Posts" area at the end of each blog post to guide readers back to prior material. This will increase reader engagement.
Respond to comments	Always respond to comments on the blog and when you detect a mention on another blog, thank that blogger in the comments of the post. This is good blogging etiquette and will help turn visitors into loyal readers.
Cite sources	When making blog posts, always cite the source with a link and do not be afraid to mention popular bloggers by name.
LINKING PRACTICES	
Short, meaningful link URLs	The best URL structure for blogs is to be as short as

	possible while still containing enough information to make an educated guess about the content you find on the page. Avoid the 10 hyphen, lengthy blog titles that are the byproduct of many blog plug-ins.
Link appropriately in posts	When linking out in your blog posts, use convention where applicable and creativity when warranted, but be aware of how the links you serve are part of the content you provide. Not every issue you discuss or site you mention needs a link. There is a fine line between overlinking and underlinking. Think of the post from the standpoint of a relatively uninformed reader. If you mention *Wikipedia*, everyone is familiar with the site and no link is required. If you mention a specific page at *Wikipedia*, a link is necessary and important. Also, be aware that quoting other bloggers or online sources (or even discussing their ideas) without linking to them is considered bad etiquette and can earn you scorn that could cost you links from those sources in the future. It is almost always better to be over-generous with links than under-generous.
Build a substantive blogroll	Identify authoritative blogs, websites, and hubs for outbound resource links and blogrolls. Look for interesting blogs that cover similar topics as yours, and then enter their links on your blogroll. When your readers click on the links, those on your blogroll can see that they are getting traffic from your blog. It works the same way when you link to other blogs within your posts. It is another way of letting the community know you are there and interested in what they are saying. Some of the sites on your blogroll might even reciprocate by putting you on their blogroll.
Reward inbound links	Often used as a barometer for the success of a blog, as well as a website, inbound links are paramount to an elevation in search results and overall rankings. To encourage more of them, make it easy and provide clear rewards. Similarly, listing blogs that have recently linked to you provides them with the reward of visibility.
COMMUNITY	
Comment on other blogs	Set a goal to post thoughtful comments on at least three to five blogs a week. If this sounds like too much to you, start out with a less ambitious goal. The important thing is to get into the habit of commenting on other blogs. Look for interesting blogs in your genre, as a way to keep current with your subject area. When one of their posts catches your eye,

	post a relevant comment. (Research posts within your genre at *Technorati*.) When you post, leave your full name rather than posting anonymously. Also include a link to the URL of your blog. This will help you build name recognition within these communities.
Use trackbacks	Trackbacks are an effective means of making connections within the blogging community. A trackback is like leaving a remote comment on a person's blog. When referencing a post on another blog, use the trackback address for that post and link to it in your post. When creating a trackback to someone else's post, an excerpt from your post, including your URL, appears below theirs in the trackback area.
Reward helpful users	Often helpful or popular users will be influencers and champions within your blogging community. Devise ways to elevate them by promoting their works on your blog's homepage, or develop a rating system. Sometimes a quick e-mail or note in private telling them you appreciate them can go a long way.
Participate in related forums	No matter what industry or niche you belong to, there are bloggers, forums, and other online communities that are already active. Depending on the specificity of your focus, you may need to think one or two levels broader than your own content to find a large community, but with the size of the participatory web today, even the highly specialized content areas receive attention. A great way to find out who these people are is to use *Technorati* to conduct searches, then sort by number of links to their blogs. This is a measure of blog *authority*. The *authority* of a blog is determined in part by the number of inbound links. A blog with many links pointing to it, especially from sites that also have many inbound links, will have more authority than a similar site with fewer inbound links.
BLOG MANAGEMENT	
Organize archives with categories	The best archives are typically organized into subjects and date ranges. For traffic referred from search engines (such as Google and Yahoo!), it is best to offer the full content of every post in a category on the archive pages. From a usability standpoint, just linking to each post is far better, possibly with a very short snippet. Balance these two issues and make the decision based on your goals.
Monitor your metrics	Visitor tracking software can tell you which posts the audience likes best, which ones do not get viewed and how

	the search engines are delivering traffic. Use these clues to react and improve your strategies. Consider adding action tracking to see what sources of traffic are bringing the best quality visitors, in terms of time spent on the site and number of page views.
Build your brand	One of the most important aspects of blogging is brand-building. A great brand needs to be a brand with which people want to be associated. People should feel that they derive something of value from their membership. Exclusivity, insider jokes, e-mails with regulars, and references to your previous experiences may put off new readers, but they are a good way to keep loyal readership feeling positive about their brand experience. Be careful to stick to your brand. Once you have a definition that people like and are comfortable with, it is very hard to break that mold without repercussions. Refer back often to the goals of your blog and the attributes of its identity to help remind you as you write.

Appendix C
Keyword Research

The Importance of Keywords

Keywords and phrases are important because individuals usually find your blog as a result of entering them into a search engine. Search engines such as Google determine the suitability of a search result by analyzing the following components of your blog:

- Title of the blog
- Post titles
- Content within posts and on other pages of the blog
- Category labels

The more consistent you are in your use of keywords and phrases throughout your blog, the greater the likelihood of ranking higher in search results for those terms over time. This will help jumpstart your readership-building strategy significantly.

Keyword Research Process

Below are some basic steps that will help you identify keywords that are aligned with your topic area and have a sufficient level of popularity as search terms that you can use them to attract readers.

Create a starter list of terms that you think capture important aspects of your topic. These can be drawn from books, magazines, trade journals, related websites or just your own personal knowledge and experience base.

Enter these into a keyword research tool (see the list in the next section) and note the number of searches made using these terms during the last 30 days. Depending on how general the term, you may see anything from no searches to millions. While it might be tempting to think about using terms with lots of searches, this can be a problem. It means you have lots of competition from other sites using those terms. Try to find terms that have an intermediate number of searches (say in the low to mid thousands). This will give your site more of an opportunity to appear with a higher ranking in the search results over time.

Most keyword research tools will provide alternative, but related, keywords or phrases for you to consider. You may discover new ways that people are thinking about and trying to get information on your topic. If these look reasonable, add them to your list. You can include them in your posts later.

Try out searches on the blog search engines to see what kind of search results are produced. Discard search terms that generate too many off-topic results. You may think the term is appropriate, but if it does not group you with similar sites, it will not help you build readership.

The last step is to narrow down your list to a reasonable number, say 30-50 terms. For each term, make a list of the blogs that appear near the top of the search results. Once you have narrowed down the list of your search terms, make a list of these blogs filtered by authority (see the Glossary). These are the blog neighbors you ultimately want to link to you.

Keyword Research Tools

There are many excellent tools to help you find good keywords and phrases to use in your blog. See the names and URLs of several popular tools below. Be sure to periodically check the websites of these tools as their features are being constantly updated.

The most popular paid keyword research services include:

- Keyword Discovery (http://www.keyworddiscovery.com)
- Wordtracker (http://www.wordtracker.com)
- Overture (http://www.overture.com)

- Digital Point keyword suggestion tool
  (http://www.digitalpoint.com/tools)
- Google keyword research tool
  (https://adwords.google.com/select/Keyword
  ToolExternal)
- Niche Bot (http://www.nichebot.com)

If you are blogging on a tight budget, there are a number of free keyword research tools including:

- SEOBook keyword suggestion tool
  (http://tools.seobook.com/general/keyword)
- Good Keywords (http://www.goodkeywords.com)
- Keyword Spider (http://www.keywordspider.com)
- Keyword Tumbler (http://www.keywordtumbler.com)

Appendix D
Blog Metric Services

There are a number of excellent blog metric services available and most of them are either free or offer free account packages. Below are eight such tools, with a brief description of each.

MeasureMap. *MeasureMap* has a better interface than *Performancing Metrics*, offers an RSS feed for metric data and has a visually pleasing data presentation. However it has some limitations. *MeasureMap* does not provide data on visitors' screen resolution, it does not track *AdSense* clicks, and it is more complicated to integrate into a blog design.

Google Analytics. *Google Analytics* is not a blog-specific metrics solution. It is a free website metrics solution that came out of *Urchin*. It offers a lot of data from traffic referrals to number of visits and page views to the ratio of new readers to returning readers to visitor loyalty, the number of visits done by website readers. Installation is easy, and reports are divided into sections: *Executive, Marketer,* and *Webmaster.* In the *Webmaster Overview*, you have page views and visits for the last four days, new vs. returning visitors, and visit by source all displayed on graphs. You have the ability to see which posts are being viewed the most as well. Also, if you want to further customize your posts for an audience, then you can look at web browsers, operating systems, screen sizes and more. It is web-based, but if you wish, you can print and export reports.

Crazy Egg. *Crazy Egg* is a different type of metrics system as it monitors where your readers are clicking and superimposes this on a screen capture of your website design. It also generates a "heat map" which shows a small picture of your blog screens with color areas indicating where your readers are clicking. Some of these data are intuitive: readers click on menu items, for example. But it also helps you spot interface items ignored by readers.

Site Meter. *Site Meter* is a free, easy to use blog counter service. It provides you with metrics such as: how many people visit your site, where they came from, how many pages they viewed and how long they stayed in the site. It also now tracks the links readers click to leave your blog.

Map Surface. *Map Surface* tracks where people linked to your site and which links they click to leave it. It offers less traffic data than *Site Meter* and less user activity data than most of the metric services above. *Map Surface* data is public and you can just press ALT + X at the *Map Surface* site to load and check the data collected by the service.

Sitening. For many blogs, visitors from search engines constitute a large part of their overall traffic. If you are serious about increasing your readership, you have to track your ranking in search results pages so you will have a better idea of how to optimize your site. You can manually monitor your ranking by searching in the different search engines using keywords you want to target. *Google*, being the most used search engine, should be your first stop. *Sitening* automates the monitoring of your *Google* search results ranking. The *Sitening* tracker service is free and its SERP Tracker allows you to track unlimited domains and unlimited keywords.

To start tracking keywords, enter your domain name and then start entering keywords or phrases. When entering keywords or phrases, you can specify whether these words will be checked daily, weekly or monthly. You can also specify the "search depth," from just checking whether you are in the top 10 results to digging deeper up to the top 100 results. Checking up to the top 100 results will need 10 queries. The *Sitening* search results tracker presents your ranking in a graph format and shows you whether you are trending higher or lower in the results pages of your targeted keywords.

103Bees. *103bees* gives your website numbers and more, much more. It tells you how people get to your site, from which search engine, and what search phrase. It lists how many visitors came to your site via specific search engines. It also tells you your top landing pages, search terms, and keywords.

Clicky. *Clicky* is a new website metrics tool that will help you track visitor sessions, how website visitors found your site, how long they stayed and the last page they viewed before leaving. *Clicky* does the usual tracking of unique visitors and page views as well as browsers used and search engine and keyword referrals.

But what differentiates *Clicky* from many of the other free services is that it tracks visitor sessions. A session is a record of an individual's stay on your blog or site, from the time they enter to the time they leave. The service provides a summary of each session, such as how long they stayed, how many pages they viewed, where they came from, as well as their entry and exit pages.

Appendix E
Self-Publishing Companies

There are many companies available now to help you self-publish your book. The services and pricing plans offered by these companies vary widely so study the information they have on their websites carefully before deciding which service is right for your needs. Some of the factors you should consider include:

Range of production services. For example, do they offer assistance with editing and design?

Marketing. Do they provide any marketing beyond simply listing your book in their catalog?

Distribution. Will they help you get your book listed with distributors and wholesalers?

Pricing. How are their contracts structured? Do you pay up front, in installments as work is completed, via royalty, or a percentage of the per unit production cost?

Approval. Do you have the ability to check and approve work in progress? Is there a well-understood process for correcting errors, and if an error is made by the publishing house, do they fix it at their cost or yours?

The standard (and probably the most comprehensive) reference for self-publishing your book is Dan Poynter's classic, *The Self-Publishing Manual : How to Write, Print, and Sell Your Own Book, 15th Ed. (Self-Publishing Manual).* It contains virtually everything you need to produce, market and sell your self-published work.

A good reference for evaluating self-publishing plans and contracts is *The Fine Print of Self-Publishing: The Contracts & Services of 48 Major Self-Publishing Companies--Analyzed, Ranked & Exposed* by Mark Levine, which you can find on

Amazon.com.   Below is a short list of companies that helps authors self-publish their books.

- **Lulu** (www.lulu.com). Publish and sell books, images, and other digital content online free of charge. Users can upload content, set a price, and retain control of their work.

- **iUniverse.com** (www.iuniverse.com). Services include cover and book design, an author's web page, and book sales.

- **AuthorHouse** (www.authorhouse.com). Providing premier self-publishing and marketing services.

- **Xlibris** (www.xlibris.com). Writers' resources, self-publishing, and publishing-on-demand technologies and services from this Random House Ventures strategic partner.

- **Yahoo! Publisher Network** (publisher.yahoo.com). Offering unique products and services to publishers of all sizes, the Yahoo! Publisher Network can help publishers generate additional revenue to their site.

- **Trafford Publishing** (www.trafford.com). Retail outlet for organizations and authors using on-demand publishing services. (www.trafford.com)

- **Blurb** (www.blurb.com). Offers the Booksmart software program which allows for the creation and publishing of books through a step-by-step interface.

- **Buybooksontheweb.com**   (www.buybooksontheweb.com). Stores manuscripts electronically to be published on demand.

- **InstantPublisher.com** (www.instantpublisher.com). Offering books, printed materials, and services to help writers self-publish manuscripts online, straight from the computer to the bookshelf.

- **Infinity Publishing** (www.infinitypublishing.com). Services include fulfillment and monthly royalties.

- **Outskirts Press** (www.outskirtspress.com). Offering premium publishing and distribution services, using digital publishing-on-demand technology.

- **Recollections, Inc**. (www.myPublisher.com). Offers MyPublisher services to publish hardcover books or calendars using your photos and text.
- **Hayden-McNeil** Publishing, Inc. (www.hmpublishing.com). Custom publishing for the higher education market, including customized lab manuals, chemistry lab notebooks, etc.
- **Vantage Press** (www.vantagepress.com). Offers a specialized publishing plan.
- **Dissertation.com** (www.dissertation.com). Publish your thesis or dissertation. All submissions become available in paperbound and digital format.
- **Wheat Mark** (www.wheatmark.com). Self-publishing service which offers authors of new and out-of-print books flexible on-demand publishing services.
- **Llumina Press** (www.llumina.com). Publisher of print-on-demand and ebooks. Provides ghostwriting, editing, publishing, marketing, and other services writers need to self-publish their books.
- **Griffith Publishing** (www.hodi.com). Self-publishing and marketing services.
- **Fultus Corporation** (www.fultus.com). Provides self publishing, print-on-demand, e-books, and documentation publishing for companies and authors.

Appendix F
Blog Tour Toolkit

A blog tour is a great way to publicize and market your book to your target audience. As we see in Chapter 6, you can easily find blogs in your topic area that would be amenable to featuring you and your work in one of their blog posts.

This appendix provides the following handy tools to assist you in setting up your blog tour:

- Blog tour checklist
- Sample blog appearance request e-mail
- Sample tracking spreadsheet setup

Blog Tour Checklist

The following items are important to have prepared before you start sending out requests for appearances to blog owners.

Done?	Blog Tour Checklist Item
	TOOLS
	List of audience segments you want to reach
	Tracking spreadsheet
	Create a blog tour page on your blog or website
	Appearance request e-mail templates for each audience segment
	Author photo
	Short author bio (a couple of paragraphs should do)
	Book cover art
	Book description
	Sample interview questions with answers
	Purchase links and information
	Create a book page on your blog or website for author and book info
	Create a blog appearance announcement for use by the blog owners
	RESEARCH, SCREENING & SCHEDULING
	Create list of prospective blogs for each audience segment
	Contact blog owners to determine interest
	Schedule appearances & determine type of appearance
	Determine with blog owner how to measure impact
	Send a confirmation e-mail to each blog owner who agrees to participate
	APPEARANCE & FOLLOW-UP
	Send materials to blog owner
	Add appearance to the blog tour page on your blog or website
	Respond on comments to the blog tour post (if desired by the blog owner)
	Follow-up with blog owner on metrics associated with the blog tour post
	Put a link to each blog tour post on your own blog tour page
	Send thank you letter to each blog owner who participated in the blog tour

Sample Blog Appearance Request E-mail

Below is a brief e-mail, courtesy of Steve Weber,[37] that can serve as a template for requesting an appearance on a blog. Note: replace the items inside the "[" and "]" brackets with your text.

SUBJECT: [Author Name] as guest on [Blog Name]

Dear [Blog Owner Name],

I'm a regular reader of your blog, and I believe it's one of the best sites about [topic] because [insert a reason]. I'm writing to see if you would consider having me, [Author Name] as a guest on your blog on [date], to discuss my book, [Title].

I believe the book will be of particular interest to your readership. [Provide two or three brief benefits for the blog's readers.]

If you are interested, we could set up my appearance on your blog as an interview, a guest post by me or a book review. I will be happy to respond to comments as long as they keep coming.

I hope you'll give this a try. I've prepared a document that includes a short excerpt from the book and its cover art. You can view this and additional information at my site: [www.mysite.com]. You're free to reproduce this information on your site or provide links to it.

I'd also like to send you a complimentary review copy of the book; just let me know where to mail it.

Thanks for your consideration.

Sincerely,

[name and full contact information, including postal address and phone number]

Tracking Spreadsheet

It is important to monitor each phase of your blog tour, because it is easy to lose track of who you have contacted and what your agreements are with blog owners when you have 30, 50 or more blogs on your list. One relatively easy way to do this is with a blog tour tracking spreadsheet, which we discussed in detail in Chapter 6.

Below is a brief summary of how to set up your blog tour spreadsheet. Note that you can also set this up as in Microsoft Word or other word processing programs as a table if you are not comfortable working with spreadsheets.)

1. Create a new Microsoft Excel workbook (or something similar in your favorite spreadsheet program).

2. Create a separate spreadsheet for each audience segment you want to include in your blog tour.

3. Give each spreadsheet a title that includes the audience segment and date the spreadsheet was last updated.

4. Create the following columns. You can combine the information into fewer columns if you don't like having this many columns:

    - Blog name
    - Blog URL
    - Blog owner name
    - Blog owner e-mail address
    - Date of first contact
    - Status of request—approved, rejected, tentative
    - Date of blog appearance
    - Type of blog appearance—interview, guest post, book review
    - Materials, if any, to be sent to the author, e.g., a complementary copy of the book

5. Page views for the blog post one month after your appearance; the blog owner should be able to provide this information

6. Notes for miscellaneous information you want to track

7. An optional step is to include a spreadsheet that provides a summary of your blog tour with the following columns:

- Audience segment name
- Number of blog appearance requests
- Number of acceptances
- % acceptance rate
- Total number of page views for this audience segment
- % of total blog tour page views contributed by this audience segment

The information on the summary spreadsheet can give you valuable marketing information about which audience segments respond best to your book.

Appendix G
Book Video Toolkit

Book videos, or book trailers as they are also known, can play an important role in attracting readers to your book. These videos convey a lot of information in an easy to digest visual format, with a potentially strong emotional appeal.

We covered the basics of creating and distributing book videos in Chapter 7. This appendix provides some tools that can help you plan, produce, and distribute your book video. These include:

- Book video checklist
- Create brief template
- Book video script template
- List of companies that specialize in producing book videos
- List of book video distribution sites

Book Video Checklist

The following checklist identifies items that are important to have prepared before you start your book video project. Note: This checklist assumes that a third party will do the video production and editing for you.

Done?	Book Video Checklist Item
	PRE-PRODUCTION
	Creative brief
	Book video script
	Treatment
	Book cover art
	Author photo & bio
	Book description
	Special graphics, illustrations or photos you want to include in the video
	Book website or blog URL
	Purchase links & information
	Contract with production team
	Identify & secure voiceover & screen talent
	Identify & secure members who will support the video shoot
	Identify & secure pecial locations & props
	Identify & secure music, B-roll or stock footage you will use
	Create budget & schedule
	Create site distribution list
	PRODUCTION
	Shoot video
	Record voiceovers
	POST-PRODUCTION
	Edit music, audio and video
	Review and approve final production master
	Transcode video to a form suitable for digital distribution via the Internet
	Distribute the video
	Monitor downloads and other metrics for each distribution site
	Link to book trailer from your book website or blog

Book Video Creative Brief Template

The purpose of the creative brief is to identify the primary audience for your book trailer, the message you will deliver to that audience segment, and your goals for the video. The questions in the template creative brief below will help you better define your book video.

1. What is the primary purpose of the book video?

2. What is unique about this author and / or the book?

3. Who are the primary and secondary audiences for the book video?

4. What is the primary motivation of each audience?

5. Describe the main idea the book video must communicate.

6. Describe the impact you want to have on the viewer or the action you want the viewer to take as a result of watching your book trailer.

7. Describe any mandatory elements such as graphics or photos that should be used in the book video and why.

Book Video Script Template

Below are two ways to create a book video script template. The first approach has the advantage of simplicity, the second, however, may be better for conveying information to a third party production team about how your book video should flow.

Approach 1—Simple Tabular Book Video Script

A tabular script is easy to set up and follow-up. It has a nice linear structure that describes the action and other elements of each scene in the book video. The tabular format is also simple to review and edit to incorporate changes to the script. To create the tabular script:

1. Set up a 4 column table in Microsoft Word or your favorite word processing program.
2. Label column 1 "#." This is the scene number.
3. Label column 2 "Time." This column will show the planned length of the segment.
4. Label column 3 "Video." This column describes the action, characters and / or graphics that will be seen by the viewer.
5. Label column 4 "Audio." This contains the voiceover narrative or what the characters onscreen are saying.

Approach 2—Storyboard Book Video Script

The storyboard has been around as long as films and videos have been made. In the past, storyboards were handcrafted on poster boards or large sheets of drawing paper. An artist would sketch out a scene and add a bit of descriptive text to describe what the scene was about. Today, you can use presentation tools to create a simple storyboard. The advantage of this approach is that it is highly visual and the elements of the storyboard can be animated to a small extent. The disadvantage is that it takes longer to create, requires more skill on the part of the person developing the storyboard, and it is difficult to edit. To create the storyboard script:

1. Open a blank presentation in Microsoft PowerPoint or your favorite presentation program.

2. Give the title screen the name of the book video.

3. Using the tools in the presentation program, create representative visuals. You can include graphics or photos you already have to simplify this process.

4. Add animation to the visual elements to illustrate the action, if you feel comfortable doing this.

5. In the notes area at the bottom of the screen (at least in PowerPoint), add the scene number, planned length (in minutes and seconds) and the voiceover or character audio script. If you did not provide animation for the visual elements, you might also want to describe the action that occurs in the *notes* area as well.

Book Video Production Companies

Below are several companies that specialize in the production and marketing of book videos:

- **Bookstream, Inc**. (www.bookstreaminc.com)
- **Circle of Seven Productions** (www.cosproductions.com)
- **Expanded Books** (www.expandedbooks.com)
- **TurnHere, Inc**. (www.turnhere.com)

Book Video Metrics

Below are some of the basic book video metrics that you can get for free from most video distribution services. A short list of the premium book video metrics that you generally have to pay for is also provided for your review.

Basic metrics

- Total views (across multiple sites)
- Number of comments
- Ratings from viewers

Premium Metrics

- Blogs and websites linking to your videos
- Audience demographics – gender, age, household income, ethnicity, education and household size
- Geographic location of the viewers watching your videos
- "Buzz" tracking – this means tracking videos and viewership across the internet based upon selected keywords; buzz includes what is being said about your video as well as other videos using similar keywords

Book Video Distribution Sites

Below are just some of the companies offering distribution services for online video online, many of them free:

5min (when applicable)	Meebo	Viddler
Addicting Clips	MeeVee	VidPow
AOL	Mefeedia	Vimeo
AtomUploads	Mixx	VSocial
Backflip	Myjeeves	Yahoo Video
Blinklist	MySPace	YouTube
Blinx	Pando	Borders
Blip TV	Photobucket	BN.com
Bluedot	Propeller	Powells.com
Break	PureVideo	Southern Independent Bookseller's Association-all bookstores
ClipBlast	Putfile	Watch the Book
Crackle	REAL	Preview the Book
DailyMotion	REC TV	DigiGirls
Del.icio.us	REC TV Blog	Dark Scribe Magazine
Digg	Reddit	TerrorFeed (Horror only)
Flickr	SearchforVideo	Romance Novel TV (Romance only)
Flurl	Sevenload	GoodReads
Folkd	Spash Cast	BooksiRead
Furl	Spurl	Ebookisle
GoFish	StumbleUpon	Night Owl Romance
Google Video	Sumo	Romance Designs Theater
Internet Archieve	Technoratti	COS Productions website and newsletter
iTunes	TotalVid	Find Me an Author
Lycos	Twitter	Kim's Wonderful World of Books
Magnolia	Veoh	OverDrive (

Appendix H
Podcasting Resources

Podcast Directories

- **Podcast Directory** is the largest user-built directory of podcasts.
- **Podcast Alley**, one of the most popular podcasting sites, has a large podcast directory.
- **Odeo.com** is a directory and podcast service
- **iPodder.org** is an established, very large podcast directory.
- **PodcastPickle** is the only podcast directory with a pickle mascot! The site features a content rating system based on the familiar movie system, G, PG, R, etc.
- **Digital Podcast**
- **PodcastDirectory com** is from Penguin Radio
- **Podcast.net**
- **iPodderX**
- **iTunes** is Apple's proprietary (non-web) directory and drives a huge amount of traffic to many podcasts
- **Yahoo!** - has a podcast search and tag-based index
- **Bipmedia.org**
- **BlogMatrix**
- **Castpost**
- **Dircaster**
- **GarageBand Podcast Studio**
- **Hipcast**

- ICanCast.com
- LibSyn
- MediaBlog
- MoveDigital
- MyPodcasts.net
- OSCDN
- Ourmedia.org
- Podblaze.com
- Podbus.com
- Podcast Spot
- PodcastSPOTS
- Podkive
- Podlot.com
- PodOmatic
- PodServe Shockpod
- Slapcast.com
- StreamGuys
- Switchpod.com

Ways to Promote Your Podcasts

Here are a few ways you can promote your podcasts online:

- Build a blog or website associated with your podcast and use the techniques of search engine optimization (SEO) and search engine marketing (SEM) to promote it

- Get listed in multiple podcast indexes

- Link to your podcasts on your profile page on social networking sites like MySpace and Facebook

- Make an announcement via online press releases on sites like PR.com

Budget Considerations for Podcasters

Below are some of the items you will need to budget for when you begin creating podcasts. The list is divided into set up costs and ongoing operating costs.

- **Set up costs**
  - Equipment
  - Software
  - Domain registration
  - Design / implementation
- **Operating costs**
  - Storage & bandwidth
  - Production costs
  - Marketing costs
  - Your time

One of the costs you will need to particularly monitor is your storage and bandwidth, especially bandwidth. The table below shows a typical cost scenario for podcasting based on the number of subscribers per month, the bandwidth they use for a typical podcast download in a month, and the overall bandwidth cost. You can see that these costs can escalate rapidly if your podcasts develop a large listener base.

Month	Subscriber Bandwidth	Number of Subscribers	Total Bandwidth	Total Monthly Cost
1	173 MB	500	86.5 GB	$ 65
2	173 MB	1,250	216 BG	$ 162
3	173 MB	1,750	302 GB	$ 227
4	173 MB	2,500	432 GB	$ 324
5	173 MB	6,600	1,141 GB	$ 855
6	173 MB	12,000	2,076 GB	$ 1,557

Glossary

Autocasting

Automated form of podcasting that allows bloggers and blog readers to generate audio versions of text blogs from RSS feeds

Audioblog

A blog where the posts consist mainly of voice recordings sent by mobile phone, sometimes with some short text message added for metadata purposes

Authority

This is determined by the number of links to a blog. A blog with many links, especially from sites that also have many inbound links, will have more authority than a similar site with fewer inbound links.

Bleg

A blog entry consisting of a request to the readers, such as for information or contributions. A portmanteau of "blog" and "beg". Also called "Lazyweb."

Blog carnival

A blog article that contains links to other articles covering a specific topic. Most blog carnivals are hosted by a rotating list of frequent contributors to the carnival, and serve to both generate new posts by contributors and highlight new bloggers posting matter in that subject area.

Blog client

Software to manage blogs from an operating system with no need to launch a web browser. A typical blog client has an editor, a spell-checker and a few more options that simplify content creation and editing.

Blog Content Management System

A tool which allows non-programmers to easily build a blog. The tool takes care of things like page structure, posts and comments, RSS feeds and the like.

BlogDay

On BlogDay (August 31st every year), bloggers from all over the world post a recommendation of five new blogs, preferably, blogs different from their own culture, point of view and attitude. On this day, blog surfers will find themselves leaping and discovering new, unknown blogs, celebrating the discovery of new people and new bloggers.

Blogger

Person who runs a blog. Also *blogger.com*, a popular blog hosting website. Rarely: weblogger.

Bloggies

One of the most popular blog awards.

Blog feed

The XML-based file in which the blog hosting software places a machine-readable version of the blog so that it may be "syndicated" for further distribution on the web. Formats such as RSS and Atom are used to structure the XML file. (See Appendix A.)

Blog hopping

To follow links from one blog entry to another, with related side-trips to various articles, sites, discussion forums, and more.

Blogorrhea

A portmanteau of "blog" and "logorrhea", meaning excessive and/or incoherent talkativeness in a weblog.

Blogroll

A list of blogs. A blogger features a list of his favorite blogs in the sidebar of his blog.

Blogosphere

All blogs, or the blogging community. Also called blogistan or, more rarely, blogspace.

Blog site

The web location (URL) of a blog, which may be either a dedicated domain, a sub-domain, or embedded within a website.

Blog tool

This refers to the software necessary to create and maintain a blog.

Blog tour

A blog tour is a set of visits to multiple blogs by an author. The owner of each blog in the blog tour interviews the author, either in a podcast or via e-mail and then publishes the interviews for his / her readers.

Blogging ahead

This is the process of creating multiple posts in advance of when they will be published and then scheduling their publication dates.

Blogsite

Sometimes confused with a simple blog or **blog site**, but a **blogsite** is a website which combines blog feeds from a variety of sources, as well as non-blog sources, and adds significant value over the raw blog feeds.

Blogsnob

A person who refuses to respond to comments on their blog from people outside their circle of friends.

Blogstorm

When a large amount of activity, information and opinion erupts around a particular subject or controversy in the blogosphere; it is sometimes called a **blog swarm.**

Blogstream

A play on the term mainstream that references the alternative news and information network growing up around weblogs and user-driven content mechanisms. Can also be used as a play on the phrase "thought-stream," referring to the stream of consciousness as expressed through a blog.

Blog Swarm

(See blogstorm)

BlogThis

Pioneered by *Blogger.com*, BlogThis links on a blog allow the reader to automatically generate a blog entry based on the blog entry he/she is reading, and post to his/her blog.

Blook

The word "blook" is a combination of blog and book. It refers to a book that has been developed with a blog as its primary source material.

Book equivalent

A measure of the amount of content, as determined by the number of books the content would equal. A typical 220 page book has about 75,000 words. A book equivalent is the total number of words in all the posts of a blog, divided by 75,000.

Bookmark

A link to a blog or blog post left on a social networking site that others can tag, i.e., add a category label that describes the blog.

Bookmarking

Bookmarking is the process of creating a bookmark for a blog (see Bookmark above).

Clashback

A heated or angry response from a blogger to a comment.

Click through

A click through occurs when a visitor to a site clicks a link to an advertisement or affiliate program.

Click through rate

The number of click throughs in a given time period.

Comment spam

Like e-mail spam. Robot "spambots" flood a blog with advertising in the form of bogus comments. This is a serious problem that requires bloggers and blog platforms to have tools to exclude some users or ban some addresses in comments.

Digg

A popular social bookmarking site (see Bookmarking above).

Dark Blog

A non-public blog (e.g., behind a firewall).

Flame war

A heated or angry exchange that takes place on a blog through its posts and comments.

Flog

A portmanteau of "fake" and "blog." A blog that is ghostwritten by someone, such as in a marketing department.

Helper plug-in

A piece of code which can be easily integrated with a blog to add more functionality, e.g., calculating blog metrics or adding an RSS feed.

Information Trap

An information trap is a tool that automatically captures or "traps" information according to a set of user specifications. A common example is the RSS feed. A user can subscribe to an RSS feed based on the results of a keyword search. The information is automatically sent to the user as it is updated.

Linkability

This term refers to the suitability of a post for linking from bookmarking sites or other blogs.

Linkbait

Linkbait is a blog post that is likely to attract attention and perhaps be bookmarked on a social networking site.

Metrics Mashup

This is the process of combining metrics from multiple sources to get a better picture of a blog's performance.

Milblog

Term for blogs written by members or veterans of any branch of service - Army, Navy, Air Force, or Marines. A contraction of *military* and *blog*

Moblog

A combination of "mobile" and "blog." A blog featuring posts sent mainly by mobile phone.

Multi-blog

Creating, maintaining, and running multiple blogs simultaneously.

Multi-blogger

An individual, business, or institution that runs multiple blogs.

Permalink

The unique URL of a single post. Use this when you want to link to a post somewhere.

Photoblog

A blog mostly containing photos, posted constantly and chronologically.

Ping

The alert in the TrackBack system that notifies the original author of a blog post when someone else writes an entry concerning the original post.

Podcasting

Contraction of "iPod" and "broadcasting" (but not for iPods only). Posting audio and video material on a blog and its RSS feed, for digital players.

Post Title Tags

These are labels which are embedded in the HTML that indicate what the content of the post is about. In blogging tools, this function is usually performed by assigning the post to categories.

RSS reader / aggregator

Software or online service allowing a blogger to read an RSS feed, especially the latest posts on his favorite blogs. Also called a reader, or feedreader. (See Appendix A.)

RSS feed

The file containing a blog's latest posts; it is read by an RSS aggregator/reader and shows at once when a blog has been updated; it may contain only the title of the post, the title plus the first few lines of a post, or the entire post. (See Appendix A.)

SEO

This acronym stands for "search engine optimization" and refers to the collection of techniques used to ensure that your site or blog always appears as high as possible in search results using certain targeted keywords.

SERP

Search engine results page. The list of results that appear when a user types keywords into a search engine.

SMO

This acronym stands for "social media optimization" which refers to the process of creating buzz and generating links to a blog on various social networking sites, e.g., MySpace.

Spiders

Spiders, also known as web crawlers, are automated programs which browse the World Wide Web in a methodical, automated manner to gather and update information on web sites for search engines.

Splog

A blog which is composed of spam. A Spam blog or any blog whose creator doesn't add value through their written content.

Slashdotted

The Slashdot effect can hit blogs or other website, and is caused by a major website (usually *Slashdot*, but also *Digg*, *Metafilter*, *Boing Boing* and others) sending huge amounts of temporary traffic that often slow down the server.

Tag cloud

A group of tags for a blog post referenced on a social networking site.

TrackBack

A system that allows a blogger to see who has seen the original post and has written another entry concerning it. The system works by sending a 'ping' between the blogs, and therefore providing the alert.

Troll

A commenter whose sole purpose is to attack the views expressed on a blog and incite a "flamewar." The troll fishes for an angry response from the blog writer and/or pro commenter. Many trolls will leave their remarks on multiple posts and continue to visit the blog, sparking spirited debate among the blog's regular readers. Troll verbosity can range from eloquent to crass, although most trolls probably fall into the latter category.

Unique View

A page view by one unique visitor to a site.

Vlog

A video blog; a vlogger is a video blogger (e.g., someone who records himself interviewing people from a certain field).

Web analytics

These are the various measurements that one can use to track the growth and impact of a blog. Examples of web analytics include page views, unique visitors, average time spent on the site, referring site, etc.

XML

Extensible markup language. This is a type of markup language (derived from the more general SGML) which describes the structure of data. This is in contrast to HTML (Hypertext Markup Language) which describes page presentation.

Bibliography

Anderson, Chris, **The Long Tail: Why the Future of Business is Selling Less of More**, Hyperion, New York, NY, 2006

Byron D.L., S. Broback, **Publish and Prosper: Blogging for Your Business**, New Riders Press, 2006

Calishain, T., **Information Trapping: Real-time Research on the Web**, New Riders, Berkeley, CA, 2007

Castro, Elizabeth, **Publishing a Blog with Blogger : Visual QuickProject Guide (Visual Quickproject Series),** Peachpit Press, 2005

Colborn, James Search, **Marketing Strategies: A Marketer's Guide to Objective Driven Success from Search Engines (Emarketing Essentials),** Butterworth-Heinemann, 2005

Demopoulos, Ted, **Secrets of Successful Blogging**, Demopoulos Associates, 2007

Farkas, Bart, **Secrets of Podcasting: Audio Blogging for the Masses**, Peachpit, Berkely, CA, 2006

Felix, L. & D. Stolarz, **Hands-On Guide to Video Blogging and Podcasting: Emerging Media Tools for Business Communication**, Focal Press, Oxford, UK 2006

Flynn, Nancy, **Blog Rules: A Business Guide to Managing Policy, Public Relations, And Legal Issues,** AMACOM/American Management Association, 2006

George, David, **The ABC of SEO**, Lulu.com, Morrisville, NC, 2005

Geoghegan, Michael & Klass, Dan, Podcast Solutions: **The Complete Guide to Podcasting**, Friedsof, 2005

Gillmor, Dan, **We the Media**, O'Reilly Media, San Francisco, CA 2004

Grappone, J. & G. Couzin, **Search Engine Optimization: An Hour a Day**, John Wiley Publishing, Inc., Indianapolis, IN, 2006

Herrington, Jack, **Podcasting Hacks**, O'Reilly Media, Sabastopol, CA, 2005

Hill, Brad, **Blogging for Dummies**, For Dummies, Foster City, CA, 2006

Ledford, Jerri, **Search Engine Optimization Bible**, John Wiley, Inc., Indianapolis, IN, 2007

Levine, Mark, **The Fine Print of Self-Publishing: The Contracts & Services of 48 Major Self-Publishing Companies--Analyzed, Ranked & Exposed**, Bridgeway Books, 2006

Mack, Steve & Ratcliffe, Mitch, **Podcasting Bible**, John Wiley, Inc., Indianapolis, IN, 2007

Meloni, Julie, **Blogging in a Snap (Sams Teach Yourself)**, SAMS, 2005

Poynter, Dan, **The Self-Publishing Manual : How to Write, Print, and Sell Your Own Book, 15th Ed. (Self Publishing Manual)**, Para Publishing, 2006

Rutledge, Patrice-Anne, **The Web-Savvy Writer: Book Promotion with a High-Tech Twist**, Pacific Ridge Press, 2006

Sabine-Wilson, Lisa, **Wordpress for Dummies**, Wiley Publishing, Inc., Indianapolis, IN, 2008

Sampson, Brent, **Sell Your Book on Amazon: The Book Marketing COACH Reveals Top-Secret "How-to" Tips Guaranteed to Increase Sales for Print-on-Demand and Self-Publishing Writers**, Outskirts Press, 2007

Scoble, Robert & S. Israel, **Naked Conversations: How Blogs are Changing the Way Businesses Talk with Customers**, John Wiley & Sons, New York, NY, 2006

Shepard, Aaron, **Aiming at Amazon: The NEW Business of Self Publishing, or How to Publish Your Books with Print on Demand and Online Book Marketing on Amazon.com**, Shepard Publications, 2007

Stauffer, Todd, **Blog On: Building Online Communities with Web Logs**, McGraw-Hill / OsborneMedia, New York, NY, 2002

Warlick, David, **Clear Blogging: How People Blogging Are Changing the World and How You Can Join Them**, Lulu.com, Morrisville, NC 2005

Walsh, Bob, **Clear Blogging: How People Blogging Are Changing the World and How You Can Join Them**, Apress, Berkeley, CA 2007

Weber, Steve, **Plug Your Book! Online Book Marketing for Authors, Book Publicity through Social Networking**, Weber Books, 2007

Wright, Jeremy, **Blog Marketing**, McGraw-Hill, New York, NY, 2005

Notes

[1] For an excellent discussion of the history of blogging, consult the Wikipedia article at
http://en.wikipedia.org/wiki/Blogging

[2] See Wikipedia, search term "Blog" for an excellent history of blogging -
http://en.wikipedia.org/wiki/Blogging#1994_.E2.80.93_2001

[3] Smith, Aaron, New numbers for blogging and blog readership, Pew Internet Posts, July 22, 2008, http://www.pewinternet.org/PPF/p/1494/pipcomments.asp

[4] Catherine Franz, writing on Publishing Central, provides an entertaining look at the hidden agendas publishers may have when considering a book for publication in her post "28 Reasons Why Publishers Will Buy Your Book." http://publishingcentral.com/articles/20051106-87-ad78.html

[5] Definition of print on demand provided by Ginny Wiehardt, on About.com,
http://fictionwriting.about.com/od/publishingterms/g/pod.htm

[6] Book industry statistics provided by Dan Poynter on his website parapublishing.com.
http://bookstatistics.com/sites/para/resources/statistics.cfm

[7] "The Twenty Five Most Valuable Blogs" March 26, 2008,
http://247wallst.com/2008/03/26/the-twenty-five/

[8] See the Nielsen BookScan website at: http://www.bookscan.com/controller.php?page=109

[9] For an in-depth description at the Espresso Book Machine, see the OnDemand Books website at: http://www.ondemandbooks.com/hardware.htm

[10] Dave Sifry, "State of the Blogosphere, October 2006", Sify's Alerts,
http://www.sifry.com/alerts/archives/000443.html

[11] Mike Eagen, "New book, blog focus on coffee shop digital nomads," Computerworld Blogs, September 28, 2008 at:
http://blogs.computerworld.com/new_book_blog_focus_on_coffee_shop_digital_nomads

[12] Free keyword discovery tools include:
- SEOBook keyword suggestion tool (http://tools.seobook.com/general/keyword)
- Good Keywords (http://www.goodkeywords.com)
- Keyword Spider (http://www.keywordspider.com)
- Keyword Tumbler (http://www.keywordtumbler.com)

[13] Blog tours usually involve an e-mail interview with an author, a review of the book and / or a guest post by the author.

[14] "Tracking Coffee House Commuter Culture – An Interview with Gregg Taylor and Lori Thiessen", Future Perfect Publishing, May 7, 2009,

http://futureperfectpublishing.com/2009/05/07/tracking-coffee-house-commuter-culture-an-interview-with-gregg-taylor-and-lori-thiessen/

15 "How many users does Twitter really have?" Mark Evans, *Twitterrati*, May 27, 2009 http://www.twitterrati.com/2009/05/27/how-many-users-does-twitter-really-have/

16 As of this writing, Cheryl Hagedorn has tracked over two hundred blog to book projects and has them indexed alphabetically and by topic on her blog Blooking Central.

17 Interview published on the Powell's Books website at: http://www.powells.com/ink/powell.html

18 *BusinessWeek (April 25, 2006) "Blooks are in Bloom" by Olga Kharif*

19 "An Interview with Podcast Novel Superstar Scott Sigler," Future Perfect Publishing, September 8, 2007. http://futureperfectpublishing.com/2007/09/08/an-interview-with-podcast-novel-superstar-scott-sigler/

20 Ibid.

21 "Podcast Novelist Extraordinarie - An Interview with 7th Son's J.C. Hutchins," Future Perfect Publishing, August, 17, 2008, http://futureperfectpublishing.com/2008/08/17/podcast-novelist-extraordinarie-an-interview-with-7th-sons-jc-hutchins/

22 Ibid.

23 Gareth Walsh and Nicholas Hellen, "Named: the Belle de Jour of the net," Times Online, March 27, 2005, http://www.timesonline.co.uk/tol/news/uk/article438397.ece

24 Juliet Lundi,"Belle de Hypothesis," 2006, http://erotic-review-coterie.blogspot.com/

25 "Diablo Cody," Wikipedia, http://en.wikipedia.org/wiki/Diablo_Cody

26 Moira Macdonald, ""Juno" writer went from stripping to Hollywood," Seattle Times, December 9, 2008, http://seattletimes.nwsource.com/html/movies/2004055219_juno09.html

27 John Scott Lewinski, "Diablo Cody's Tips for Blogging Your Way to Hollywood Success," November 16, 2007, http://www.wired.com/entertainment/hollywood/news/2007/11/cody

28 Rachel Abramowitz, "Giving Birth to Juno," LA Times, December 6, 2007, http://articles.latimes.com/2007/dec/06/entertainment/et-cody6

29 Future Perfect Publishing, "Four Quadrant Zooming - An Interview with Max Quick Series Author Mark Jeffrey," August 20, 2008, http://futureperfectpublishing.com/2008/08/20/four-quadrant-zooming-an-interview-with-max-quick-series-author-mark-jeffrey/

30 Ibid

31 Ibid

32 Ibid

33 Ibid

34 "Frank Warren," Ovation website, http://ovationtalent.com/speaker.aspx?spid=38

35 Heather Green, "The Online Fan World of the Twilight Vampire Books," BusinessWeek, July 31, 2008. http://www.businessweek.com/magazine/content/08_32/b4095044373786.htm?chan=technology_technology+index+page_top+stories

[36] "Grammar Groove – An Interview with Grammar Girl Mignon Fogarty" Future Perfect Publishing, August 3, 2007 http://futureperfectpublishing.com/2007/08/03/grammar-groove-an-interview-with-grammar-girl-mignon-fogarty/

[37] See Steve Weber's book, *Plug Your Book!: Online Book Marketing for Authors.*

W

X

Y

One concept - then a story
① Share
② Positive attitude
③ Cultural Factors
④   Differing interviews
⑤ Family Factors
⑥ a society adverse to pain (bright-side)
    I know in my family

CPSIA information can be obtained at www.ICGtesting.com
Printed in the USA
LVOW090458161111

255202LV00001B/95/P